UNIVERSITY OF NORTH CAROLINA
STUDIES IN THE ROMANCE LANGUAGES
AND LITERATURES
Number 26

THE EARLY
CUADRO de COSTUMBRES
IN COLOMBIA

by

FRANK M. DUFFEY

1956
CHAPEL HILL
THE UNIVERSITY OF NORTH CAROLINA PRESS

Copyright, 1956, by
THE UNIVERSITY OF NORTH CAROLINA PRESS

The Early *Cuadro de Costumbres* in Colombia

PREFACE

Preliminary investigation for this study was done in 1942 in Bogotá, where, thanks to the cooperation of the governments of the Republic of Colombia and the United States, I was an exchange fellow under the Convention for the Promotion of Inter-American Cultural Relations (the Buenos Aires Convention). A number of persons in Bogotá were most helpful and sympathetic during my study there. Among them were Don Gustavo Uribe, an excellent counselor and friend, Don Roberto Cortázar, Don Gustavo Otero Muñoz, and Señor Pérez Ayala of the Biblioteca Nacional.

I owe a great debt of gratitude to Dr. Sturgis E. Leavitt of the University of North Carolina, whose guidance and aid have been unerring and invaluable.

This modest book probably could have been written without the help of my wife Gwen, but it would not have been nearly as much fun.

Chapel Hill, N. C.   F. M. D.

CONTENTS

Introduction	ix
I. The Earliest Sketches	1
II. The Pre-Mosaico Writers	10
José Caicedo Rojas	11
José Manuel Groot	17
Juan Francisco Ortiz	21
Rafael Eliseo Santander	24
Juan de Dios Restrepo	26
Medardo Rivas	36
III. The Mosaico Circle	46
IV. The Mosaico Writers	50
José María Vergara y Vergara	50
José Manuel Marroquín	59
José David Guarín	67
Ricardo Silva	78
Eugenio Díaz	88
Ricardo Carrasquilla	90
Manuel Pombo	95
José Joaquín Borda	99
José María Samper	102
V. Review and Appraisal	108
Bibliography	114

INTRODUCTION

The sketch of manners, or *cuadro de costumbres*, which enjoyed great popularity in Spain and considerably influenced her literature, is a foreign genre which ought to have been invented by the Spaniards, so suited was it to the Spanish disposition, character, and genius. But, in spite of Montgomery's[1] discovery of some respectable native ancestors, the sketch as Larra and Mesonero knew it seems to have got into Spain by the much-travelled route across the Pyrenees from France, where its practitioners—Victor Joseph Etienne de Jouy was the most successful of them—had apparently got the idea from *The Spectator* and *The Tatler*.

When notice of the work of the Spanish *costumbristas* first reached Colombia is uncertain, but there is good reason to believe that the popularity of Mesonero and Larra, at least, did not lag far behind their vogue in Spain. A short-lived Bogotá paper (and most Colombian papers were extremely short-lived) called *El Correo*, in October, 1839, announces the sale, in installments, of a Caracas edition of Larra's works. A December insertion reveals clearly that Larra was available in other editions, affirming that "La edición europea, incompleta i no tan bella como la de Caracas, cuesta el doble del precio de ésta. . . ." The European edition in question must be that of Repullés, done in Madrid in five volumes, 1835-1837.

El Correo has more to say on the subject of the *costumbristas*. The following curiously naive advertisement appeared in March, 1840:

> LARRA. Como actualmente se hallan en esta capital las personas notables de las provincias, que han venido a representarlas en el congreso, creemos conveniente avisarles que se hallan de venta las obras de este excelente escritor en la tienda del Sr. Ulpiano González. . . . Ellas son un modelo de soltura i gracia en el estilo entre los últimos escritores españoles. Contienen observaciones interesantes sobre costumbres semejantes a las nuestras, i sobre acontecimientos políticos que suelen repetirse en estos países. Creemos que no hai un solo amante de las bellas letras i del mérito literario que no tenga algunas noticias de *Fígaro* i del *Pobrecito Hablador*, a cuyo lado solo puede ponerse Mesonero Romanos entre los que escriben en la lengua de Castilla. . . .

Whether or not Ulpiano González, who also had Mesonero

---

[1] Clifford Marvin Montgomery, *Early Costumbrista Writers in Spain, 1750-1830* (Philadelphia: [University of Pennsylvania], 1931).

Romanos' *Panorama matritense* for sale, was successful in his gentle effort to lead the provincial politician to culture, evidence from a less interested source tells that the Spanish *costumbristas* were among the authors read and emulated in the decade of the forties. José María Samper, himself a *costumbrista*, said before the Colombian Academy in 1886:

> Las primeras obras que por aquel tiempo llegaron a nuestras manos, pertenecían a muy diversos tipos literarios; y para dar idea de su alto mérito, bastará decir que eran creaciones de Mariano José de Larra, Mesonero y Romanos, Modesto Lafuente, Bretón de los Herreros, García y Gutiérrez, Angel de Saavedra, Eugenio de Ochoa, D. José Zorrilla y Espronceda. . . . [Deseo] hacer constar aquí todo lo que el despertamiento y progreso de la literatura colombiana deben al lejano influjo de las obras españolas a que he aludido, leídas con avidez por nuestra juventud en la época a que me refiero. . . .[2]

Add to this the occasional reprinting of Spanish articles of manners in the fitful periodical press of the time and it seems reasonable to conclude that peninsular *costumbrista* work was known in Colombia at least as early as 1839 and that it enjoyed considerable popularity in the 1840's. There was a readily available model for a domestic product.

It is almost easier to trace the history of the *cuadro de costumbres* than to say what it is. Manuals of literary history help very little—their definitions are too capacious to be of value. The stars of the genre, Larra and Mesonero, do help. Larra says, in the foreword to his *El Pobrecito Hablador* in 1832:

> Consideramos la sátira de los vicios, de las ridiculeces y de las cosas, útil, necesaria, y sobre todo muy divertida. . . . Reírnos de las ridiculeces; ésta es nuestra divisa: ser leídos; este es nuestro objeto: decir la verdad; este nuestro medio. . . .[3]

Later, in reviewing the first (1835) edition of Mesonero's *Panorama matritense*, Larra suggests the importance of the newspaper in the development of the sketch and emphasizes the requirements of accurate observation, lightness of tone, grace, humor, and a rudimentary plot or narrative.[4] Mesonero, in a much later edition of his *Panorama* (1881), says in his ponderous manner just about the same things. He also pre-

---

[2] "Discurso de recepción en la Academia Colombiana," *Repertorio Colombiano*, XII (1886), 59.
[3] *Obras completas de Fígaro* (Paris: Garnier Hermanos, n. d.), I, 28.
[4] *Ibid.*, III, 88-100.

sumptuously and incorrectly declares himself the first *costumbrista* in Spain.

Montgomery, in his study of the Spanish antecedents of the *costumbrista* movement, has a good working definition:

> The *cuadro de costumbres* may be briefly defined as a short sketch or essay in prose or verse describing some contemporary type, institution, incident or fashion, such as a dandy, the lottery, a bull-fight, a country fair, etc. It usually has very slight plot or character development, and just enough narrative to hold the interest of the reader. Realistic description is a basic characteristic. A didactic purpose is evident. The essays appeared as editorials and contributed articles, often as letters to the editor, in newspapers, semi-literary or literary periodicals, and in pamphlet form.

Montgomery leaves out only two essential characteristics—informality and some variety of humor.

The late F. Courtney Tarr considered the *costumbrista* sketch in two forms—the *artículo* and the *cuadro*. The *artículo*, which flourished in the 1830's with Larra and the earliest work of Mesonero, "has a pronounced narrative or dramatic element approximating to a story or dramatic sketch with a moral or critical point or scene." The *cuadro*, of which Estébanez Calderón was the earliest exponent and which became the dominating form after the appearance of *Los españoles pintados por sí mismos* in 1843 and 1844, is "the more detailed and affectionate description of picturesque types and customs, presented primarily for their own sakes rather than for humorous or critical purposes." The *cuadro* form, which was very popular in Colombia, is based on the assumption that the scene or custom described has sufficient interest per se to make unnecessary the use of narrative or other devices, and its didactic purpose is purely informative. Tarr points out that it is the *cuadro*, not the *artículo*, which leads directly to the regional novel of manners.[5] Neither Spanish nor Colombian writers recognized the distinction between *cuadro* and *artículo*, but it is of great value in recognizing and classifying a body of material which is likely to be confusing in its volume and variety.

Commentators and collectors of *costumbrismo* in Colombia generally include a quantity of material not appropriate to the genre. Purely political articles, biographies, short stories, sen-

---

[5] "Romanticism in Spain and Spanish Romanticism," *Bulletin of Spanish Studies*, XVI (1939), 26-27.

timental anecdotes, historical narrative, and pure history appear under the label *cuadro de costumbres,* which seems often to have served as a classification embracing all forms of casual prose. However, it is not to be inferred that Colombian writers did not know what they were writing, or why. José Manuel Marroquín, one of the best Colombian *costumbristas,* explains the genre fully—even anticipating Tarr's *cuadro-artículo* division—in a manual of rhetoric written in 1889:

> Su objeto es pintar, para instrucción de los extraños y de la posteridad, las costumbres de los países en épocas determinadas.
>
> Puédense componer también con el fin de corregir lo vituperable o defectuoso que haya en dichas costumbres. . . .
>
> Un artículo de costumbres es la narración de uno o más sucesos, de los comunes y ordinarios, hecha en tono ligero, y salpicada de observaciones picantes y de chistes de todo género. De esta narración ha de resultar o una pintura viva y animada de la costumbre de que se trata, o juntamente con esta pintura, la demostración de lo malo o de lo ridículo que haya en ella; mas esta demostración han de hacerla los hechos por sí solos, sin que el autor tenga que introducir reflexiones o disertaciones morales para advertir al lector cuál es la conclusión que debe sacar de lo que ha leídi.
>
> En este género tienen cabida los caracteres, las descripciones, los diálogos y cuanto puede adornar la historia ficticia; pero todo debe dirigirse al fin propuesto, esto es, a la pintura o al vituperio de una costumbre.[6]

The nature of the sketch of manners may vary greatly, but certain characteristics are essential. The most important consideration is subject matter. Rustic or urbane customs, polite manners, national idiosyncracies, social abuses, speech habits, intimate family life, literary, cultural, or intellectual tastes, and peculiarly national or local institutions or character types are suitable matter for the *costumbrista*. His attitude toward the subject may be one of mere detached curiosity, he may express admiration or reproof, or he may exploit his material for the sake of humor alone; but, regardless of his attitude, his approach to the subject and the tone of his article must not be intense, formal, or righteous, for his primary end is to entertain. Therefore, informality and at least ostensible levity of form and style are important characteristics. Various casual literary forms are suitable for *costumbrista* use—the personal or familiar essay, the character sketch, the simple narrative,

---

[6] *Retórica y poética* (Selección Samper Ortega de Literatura Colombiana, Vol. IV; 3d ed.; Bogotá: Editorial Minerva, 1935), pp. 98-99.

the purely humorous essay, letters, objective description or exposition, unadorned and undisguised satire, or any combination of these. A didactic purpose, informative or corrective, is typical, but in the frankly humorous pieces it may be elusive.

By history, by nature, and by purpose the sketch of manners is a periodical form, and it is in the periodical press that the true variety is found. When the sketch is incorporated in a longer literary form it changes its tone, its audience, and its function, and, although it remains within the broad field of *costumbrismo*, it is no longer a genuine *artículo* or *cuadro de costumbres*.

The material in this study of the early Colombian sketch comes from many sources. Most of the articles were first examined in the periodicals in which they originally appeared, although reference may be made to a more available text of later date. Several anthologies of *costumbrismo* have supplied material, but many collected pieces have been rejected for their failure to qualify as true sketches of manners. Therefore, much material that has generally been considered *costumbrista* has been omitted. Some articles that have escaped the collectors and critics have been included.

Limitations of space, and sometimes unavailability of material, have prevented consideration of the total *costumbrista* production of every author. However, the articles treated here are believed to be sufficiently representative to justify an estimate of the quality and importance of each author and an appraisal of the *costumbrista* movement as a whole.

The Early *Cuadro de Costumbres* in Colombia

I

THE EARLIEST SKETCHES

Some of the earliest Colombian papers disappoint the investigator in search of *costumbrista* articles. For example, *El Cachaco de Bogotá,* issued in 1833 and 1834 by Florentino González and Lorenzo M. Lleras, has a saucy title in the tradition of *costumbrista* titles and pseudonyms, but its promise is barren. Its stiffly censorious editorials on coquetry, political spoils, and spurious urbanity belie the paper's sprightly title and, though they show a disposition to criticize manners, fall far short of the *costumbrista* manner.

In 1838 a genuine *artículo de costumbres* appeared in the "Remitidos" section ("letters to the editor") of *El Argos* (number 36, July 29, 1838), a political weekly brought out for over a year and a half by Juan de Dios Aranzazu, Lino de Pombo, Rufino Cuervo, and Ignacio Gutiérrez Vergara. The article is signed with an unidentifiable pseudonym—*Quintín*—and since it appears as a *remitido* it is probably not the work of any of the editors, two of whom later wrote *costumbrista* articles. The title is "Fiestas" and the subject is extravagance and overindulgence, and their dire results, during the July 20 celebration of the anniversary of Nueva Granada's (Colombia's) uneasy independence.

Quintín's troubles begin with costumes, for his wife Tiburcia, "traviesa i retozona, aunque ya frisa en los 40 julios," insists that all must be new, elegant, and costly. The result is startling (as are the names of the children):

> Remedaba el [disfraz] de Etelredo el vestido del emperador de Marruecos, i el de Tibur-Bec el del príncipe de Beluchinán. Tiburcia vestía de sultana, i no parecía sino que había nacido en el serrallo: sus hijas, una de reina indiana, otra de princesa ejipcia, Tegualda a la española antigua, i Euridice de pastora suiza. Para mí hicieron un vestido de Arlequín, que cuantos lo vieron, alabaron el acierto i la inventiva de Tiburcia.[1]

The entertainment is as extravagant as the costuming. For Quintín and his family every hour is a century of ecstasy—"Toros, encierros, orquestas, canciones, cohetes, dulces, globos,

---

[1] The irregularities and inconsistencies in spelling and accentuation in some of the texts quoted in this study are the result of orthographic reforms enthusiastically espoused in some of the Spanish American countries just after the break with Spain.

etc., nada perdimos." Four days of revelling leave only pleasant memories, Quintín thinks, but he is awakened on July 24 by a boisterous mob of bill collectors. He flees the house in search of a money-lending friend who offers the needed money magnanimously—good security and a modest twenty per cent per month in interest. Quintín ultimately is dragged off to jail, "sin esperanza de ver otra vez la esplendente luz del sol."

"Fiestas" easily meets the requirements of an *artículo de costumbres*. It treats of contemporary manners, it has humor, the narrative is dramatically developed and well told, and the satire —on social extravagance, fair-weather friends, money-lenders, and, above all, on bad taste—gives it a clearly didactic air in spite of its frivolity of manner. It is significant that "Fiestas," as the earliest Colombian sketch of manners, is also the prototype of a particular form of *costumbrismo* which Colombians favored. This kind of personal essay, written in a tone of self-deprecation about the author's embarrassment in a series of elaborately exaggerated incidents, became one of the standard *costumbrista* vehicles. This article is a worthy beginning. Its message is not sensational nor is its technique perfect, but it is genuinely humorous and entertaining, which is more than can be said for many later articles.

Gustavo Otero Muñoz, who never saw or was unimpressed by "Fiestas," cites as the first examples of Colombian *costumbrismo* two articles by Rufino Cuervo in *El Argos* in May, 1839, ten months after the appearance of "Fiestas."[2] Rufino Cuervo (1801-1853) was a journalist, lawyer, politician, educator, and the father of Colombia's famed grammarian, Rufino José Cuervo.

The first of the Cuervo articles does not qualify at all. It is a *leyenda histórica*, a purportedly true account of a 1685 love intrigue. The second, "Un representante al congreso de 1837," deals in true *costumbrista* fashion with a simple provincial who has the misfortune to be elected to congress and suffers incredibly from unscrupulous landladies, politicians, and plain bad luck before he abandons the capital, saying: "Pobre regreso a mi tierra, pero rico en desengaños." Whether Cuervo was deploring provincial naiveté or condemning the legislative processes, his satire is effective in spite of occasional preaching,

---

[2] "El costumbrismo en Colombia," *Santafé y Bogotá*, XIII (1930), 355-358.

but his style is ponderous and suffers from an inverted syntax presumably calculated to be mock-heroic. However, the article is successful enough to stand with the more sprightly "Fiestas" as one of the earliest specimens of native *costumbrismo*.

Colombia's first sustained effort at periodical *costumbrismo* is found in *El Observador*, a Bogotá weekly by the same four men who edited *El Argos*. It ran through thirty-eight numbers beginning on September 22, 1839. Its section of "Miscelánea" often carried a sketch by José Gutiérrez Vergara (1806-1877), a statesman, politician, economist, and perennial editor.

The earliest of the series are of dubious value and may not even be full-blown *costumbrismo*. The first, in the first number of the paper, "¿Escribamos un periódico?" relates whimsically the circumstances of the founding of the weekly and concludes with the confession that the author wrote the piece only to fill space. The second article, "Mis opiniones políticas," is also of scant interest.

The third, on October 6, 1839, is better. It is a curious omnibus containing the undeveloped nuclei of four different sketches. The opening portion criticizes second-guessers in politics—"mui fácil es murmurar; pero gobernar... mui difícil." The next touches elegantly dressed but bad-mannered young men (they stand at the church door to watch the girls emerge after mass!), concluding that "la libertad de ideas ha hecho nacer... el libertinaje de costumbres." The third section comes closest to a real sketch by reproducing a conversation in which two young women characterize the men they flirt with. The last part divides marriages into two classes—*al contado* and *a plazos*—and warns that the terms of the latter are not likely to be easy. This multiple article, called "Observaciones," shows that Gutiérrez Vergara is pointed toward real *costumbrismo*, a goal he reaches with his next effort.

On October 20 Gutiérrez published "Cachaco," in which he explains through excellent type sketches the meaning of this native Colombian term. His incisive characterizations deserve quoting in part. He calls the first the primitive *cachaco*.

> Un joven raizal o de provincia, travieso i perdulario, que está en colejio a rienda corta en esto de las espensas suministradas por un acudiente un poco cicatero; que asiste a la aula dos días, i el resto de la semana está paseando o en el cepo...; que tiene siempre las manos pavonadas i las uñas como guardilla de es-

quela para convite de entierro, amén de la cara i las orejas que sólo han conocido de vista i no de trato i comunicación los dominios del dios Neptuno; que usa siempre el pelo como la conciencia de un escribano, i el sombrero como las banderas de Pizarro . . .; que sabe ocultar tantas miserias bajo de una capa o capote cuyo color primitivo se ignora, pero cuyo forro puede resistir cualquier aguacero al favor de los diferentes barnices de que está impregnado . . .; que pelea con todos sus condiscípulos, i es guapetón, i enamorado, i carga piedras i dulces i pólvora en los bolsillos; i por último, que lleva filos de doctor, en cuya carrera lo ha puesto su padre para que vaya pronto a ser notabilidad haciendo escritos o matando gente en su provincia; este joven tal es lo que se llama un *cachaco*, genuinamente dicho, con título espedido en toda forma de derecho.

The *cachaco de moda* is described with less accent on the dark tones, but no less vigorously:

¿No veis aquel otro, que es el reverso del anterior? Miradlo, ¡qué elegancia! Pera i bigotito cuidadosamente cortado a medio labio, i favoritas. . . . Parece que su madre lo parió con la casaca que lleva puesta; no se le hace una sola arruga; i los calzones i el chaleco, i la corbata, i el sombrero, no hai pero que ponerles . . .; vamos, es un Adonis; i ¡como huele! ¡qué fragancia, qué atmósfera tan perfumada va dejando por donde quiera que imprime su lijera planta! . . . Este joven, así como lo veis, esta estudiando; cursa ocho facultades distintas, i le sobra tiempo para todo; dentro de dos meses se graduará de doctor; antes de concluirse este año será abogado, i hace apenas uno que acabó filosofía; ¡tiene tanto talento! i será un prodijio cuando tome la palabra en una cámara lejislativa. . . .

But this young man soon changes classification:

Mas he aquí que ya concluyó su carrera literaria; i no comoquiera, sino que es médico i abogado, o abogado i médico en una sola pieza: un galgo no corre tanto detrás del venado, como nuestro joven adelante de los estudios. . . . Lo que ahora se trata de averiguar es, ¿cómo pasará la "vida"? Hora mozo todavía, dos profesiones, con fama de talento, ¿qué más quiere? El hombre va a comer a dos carrillos. Pero, ¡qué chasco! Los doctores en esta tierra dan ya por más arriba de la cincha, i como según el principio de los economistas la abundancia de su jénero disminuye la demanda, esta mercancía ha perdido mucho de su valor o se ha vuelto *hueso*, como dicen los comerciantes. . . . Petardo aquí, préstamo allá, así se pasan algunos días, hasta que al fin concluye nuestro heroe solicitando un destinito de escribiente de oficina. Entre tanto se enamora por la centésima vez, contrae matrimonio *a plazo*, y ya sabemos cuáles son las consecuencias. Este es un *cachaco capuchino*.

Other varieties are briefly sketched. The *cachaco de tienda*, his youth gone, spends day and night in *tertulia* in his favorite store. The *cachaco de bonete* is the negligent priest whose "costumbres personales no están en armonía con la palabra evanjélica que de vez en cuando predica." The friar who, hanging up his habit and forsaking penance and prayer, goes out by night to indulge the flesh is the *cachaco de cogulla*. The author refrains from comment on the military *cachaco* out of fear, he says, and keeps silent about the female variety for gallantry's sake. Thus the piece ends rather lamely.

"Cachaco" is a distinguished beginning for the satirical type sketch in Colombia. One may finish the reading without knowing exactly what *cachaco* means, but he will have been entertained and instructed. This article is closely similar in subject, development, and tone to Larra's "Los calaveras." Gutiérrez may have been imitating.

"Gorrista" (October 27), after a long and digressive introduction, poses a riddle: "En qué se parecen los papeles públicos a un cigarro i a una narigada de rapé?" After a number of amusing wrong answers—for example, "Se parecen al cigarro en que se vuelven humo, i al rapé en que hacen fluir toda clase de inmundicias"—Gutiérrez supplies the correct one. *"Gorrista,"* he says, "se llama al que fuma tobaco i toma rapé a costa ajena, i *gorrista* también al que lee papeles públicos sin que le cuesten nada." Gutiérrez' justified complaint (his circulation must have been pitifully small) did not solve the problem of the parasitic reader, for twenty years later a Bogotá printer irascibly declared that he would by no means accommodate the *gorrista* by depositing his papers in the National Library on the day of their publication. Gutiérrez concludes his good-humored article with the hope that his present reader is reading a copy he has paid for. He achieves an effect of cleverness in spite of having worked too hard for it.

As in "Observaciones," Gutiérrez again combines heterogeneous material in "Duelo. Duelo o catamiedo" (November 3). He deals first with *duelo* in its sense of "mourning," recounting, as many have done before and since, the strange requirements of man's concept of a "decent" burial. The second part, unconnected, concerns *duelo* as a duel, a "trajicomedia, pitipieza, o juego parecido a la golosa," and has considerable historical interest. In some duels, he says, the pistols are loaded without ball and the duelists fire into the air "en presencia de dos cirujanos, que seguramente asisten en clase de hombres buenos para

averiguar con la tienta i el escalpelo los efectos que la detonación haya causado en la atmósfera."
However,
> El uso más reciente es que los padrinos carguen las pistolas en el campo con aire grave i amenazador, pasando cien veces las balas por las narices a los dos primeros galanes del drama, i añadiendo algunas espresiones lúgubres que suenan en el oído de los pacientes como en el de Sancho el ruido de los batanes. . . .

This treatment quickly induces apologies and reconciliation.

Such farcical duels are used, says Gutiérrez, by debtors to elude payment and students to avoid failure in exams, "aunque sean unos topos." This may be true. The piece is strongly written—the amiability of "Gorrista" laid aside—and the humor is bitter. The second part would be an excellent *artículo* if it were more carefully and fully developed. Without that it is still an effective and entertaining condemnation of obnoxious practices.

"La peste" (November 17) is a high spot in the series. The *peste* is a respiratory malaise, probably the "flu," which is indispensable to the *bogotano* as a topic of conversation and a credible excuse for evasion of obligation.

> Encuéntrase una señora con otra a quien le está debiendo visita, i la dice:
> "¡Oh! mi *seá* Marcela, qué milagro es verla; ¿no ha llegado por su casa la *peste*? En la mía todos han estado mui malos: Pedrito, Joaquina, Ricarda, han caído a un mismo tiempo, i después dos criadas una tras de otra; pero ¡qué accidentes, qué calentura! Si ya estoi desesperada! . . . Por eso es que no he tenido el gusto de ver a U.; pero luego que pase la *peste*, le ofrezco ir una tarde entera."

But the *peste* never passes, of course, and its value as a justification for self-indulgence and sloth is perennial and unrestricted. "La peste" is a well-elaborated article, one of the few in which Gutiérrez uses his material to maximum effect. The introduction is brief but adequate, the conversations of the body of the article are realistically lively, and the conclusion is satirically imaginative.

On December 29, 1839, *El Observador* carried a timely sketch by Gutiérrez called "El aguinaldo," which describes a typical day of festivity at Christmas, a great season, says the author, for women, children, and *cachacos*. Beginning at six everybody goes to mass, not once but three times, and in three different churches.

Los muchachos se apoderan de los pitos para imitar el canto de
los pájaros i atronar la iglesia que quisieran convertir en el
arca de Noé; las mujeres vuelven la cara con tanta boca abierta
hacia el coro para oír los villancicos, en que a veces se representa una comedia mística, perteneciente al jénero romántico
más bien que al clásico.

Breakfast follows mass, and most of the rest of the day is spent in preparation for the night's ball.

Los alféreces se han portado como caballeros; ningún gasto
han omitido para oscurecer a sus predecesores, i tan pródigos en
la galantería como en los preparativos de la fiesta, han agotado
los recursos del lucimiento i provisto una abundante despensa,
en que se encuentran bizcochitos i dulces de todas clases para
obsequiar a las niñas, i vinos i licores para los jóvenes aficionados.

The ballroom floor is crowded. A near riot occurs during the selection of a couple to lead the *contradanza* and the general struggle for preferred position in the order of the dance. After midnight the ball becomes gayer and more martial, for "en las cabezas de muchos jóvenes suelen ocupar los vapores del brandy el lugar en que poco antes reinaba la más escarmentada galantería."

Así pasan nueve noches seguidas con más o menos modificaciones, en diferentes sociedades de los cuatro barrios de la
ciudad, terminándose la última con la misa de gallo, i una buena
cena que costea el postrer alférez.

The article was hastily composed and ends abruptly, and the modern reader might wish for more detail in the accounts of the mass and the dance; but, although the subject deserved better treatment, "El aguinaldo" is a satisfactory *cuadro* and the only article of the *Observador* series which is not critical or satirical.

On January 12, 1840, the Gutiérrez article in *El Observador* returns to a subject he had touched in the first part of his "Duelo," the extravagance and hypocrisy that accompany death and mourning, and this time he turns out a fully-developed sketch titled "Luto."

His introduction remarks on the mortal's reluctance to accept the inevitability of his own death—even the grave-digger, he says, is convinced that he will bury every member of his generation. We must die, to be sure, but we can enjoy the prospect by anticipating the ridiculous manner of our being laid to rest. Here are the trappings required:

Doscientas boletas impresas se reparten, convidando a las esequias; se cubre de cera la iglesia, desde el altar hasta la puerta;

la música, el canto, vijilia i misas; la mortaja de San Francisco que cuesta diez pesos, último precio; el cajón forrado en tela negra más o menos rica, con tachuelas doradas; las licencias del cura i de la policía, que a fuerza de regatear se consiguen la una en nueve pesos i la otra en veinte; el carrito mortuario, la bóveda, la cal, el sepulturero, el epitafio, todo esto supone gastos i recursos, además de lo que suele pagarse por la impresión de una necrolojía; i gracias a que los convidados no cobran todavía derechos de asistencia, pues si los cobraran entonces sí los entierros serían concurridos.

Gutiérrez passes from funeral manners to the paradoxical vanity practiced by women in mourning dress and concludes with a whimsical plan for regulating the degree and duration of mourning—for fathers and sons a year, for brothers six months, for uncles two, etc. This is sensible, he insists, "porque a cada uno le gustaría saber de una manera fija lo que harán sus dolientes después de que lo dejen en el cementerio." Let the immortal soul go to glory with its mortal curiosity satisfied!

Taken as a whole, Gutiérrez Vergara's pioneer series of articles in *El Observador* is completely satisfactory only historically. Though the quality is uneven and the technique unsure, the articles represent the first sustained attention by a Colombian to the *costumbrista* genre. It is not likely that Gutiérrez took these pieces very seriously. *El Observador*, a paper for which he was one-fourth responsible, was not primarily a literary journal and the "Miscelánea" section in which the articles appeared must have been considered simply trimming for the paper's more serious business, the fomentation of non-partisan patriotism.

Most of the articles show evidence of the author's casual attitude, and a few of them are admittedly space-fillers. Their greatest defect is lack of organization and orderly development. Only in "Cachaco" (and here there is an unfortunate anticlimactic arrangement), "Gorrista," and "Luto" does it seem that the author was writing with a preconceived plan. Only once— in "La peste"—does he come close to the honored *costumbrista* device, which was used, by the way, by his predecessor Quintín, of participation by himself or by an imaginary individual in an illustrative incident as a vehicle for criticism of manners. So it may be fairly concluded that Gutiérrez was a beginner in form as well as in time.

The style of the pieces is uneven and varied, but it is usually adequate. His vocabulary is extensive, he refrains from punning, his figures of speech are normally imaginative and satirically effective. Best of all, he is genuinely humorous. His humor and his almost frivolous detachment from his subject mark him a real *costumbrista*. Most of his articles can be read with real pleasure.

It is impossible to say whether Gutiérrez was influenced by Spanish *costumbristas*. Otero Muñoz says he was not:

> Siguió un camino que ninguno pisó antes ni después de él. . . . "Cachaco" . . . y "El aguinaldo" en particular no deben nada a nadie . . . y distan muchas millas de los sencillos cuadros de don Rufino [Cuervo] y de las malignas sátiras en que se desahogó el atrabiliario maestro Fígaro.³

Probably Otero Muñoz is being rashly patriotic, for it is precisely in the two articles he cites that Gutiérrez' subject and manner most suggest Larra and Mesonero. The works of both Spaniards were available to him, and it would seem less rash to adduce influence than to deny it. The best argument for Otero Muñoz' view is that if Gutiérrez was imitating he was not imitating very skillfully.

---

³ "El costumbrismo en Colombia," p. 401.

II
THE PRE-MOSAICO WRITERS

Colombia's history was tumultuous from the moment of her first break with the Spanish crown in 1810. In 1815, after initial revolutionary successes, the patriots suffered the humiliation of a brutal reoccupation of the liberated territory by royal troops under the hard-handed General Morillo. Finally the Liberator Bolívar came from Venezuela and assured Colombian independence by his victory at Boyacá in 1819. For a decade Bolívar toiled to solidify his dream of a great northern nation —Gran Colombia—but at his death in 1830 the impractical experiment was abandoned and the territory the Liberator had held together became the modern republics of Venezuela, Colombia, and Ecuador.

From 1832 to 1863 Colombia was known as Nueva Granada, the name of the colonial viceroyalty, and its first president was the statesman Francisco de Paula Santander. Under Santander there were threats of revolt but no fighting, and the new nation experienced a short period of peace marked by progress in education and industry. The peace was broken in 1840 by a disastrous civil war and no recovery could be undertaken until the regime of Tomás Cipriano Mosquera, who was elected president in 1845. There was no widespread fighting thereafter until 1860, when Mosquera himself led a devastating liberal revolt. From then until the end of the century Colombia suffered serious wars about every ten years, with incidental fighting and unrest in between. Her history in the twentieth century was relatively peaceful until the so-called Liberal revolt of 1948 and the subsequent return of the old chaos.

Political history inevitably affected Colombia's literary history. The early interest in literature—and in *costumbrismo*— and the publication of periodicals (*El Correo, El Argos, El Observador*) to reflect that interest were facilitated by the period of calm and security under the presidencies of Santander and his successor, José Ignacio Márquez, in the 1830's. *El Observador* expired in May, 1840, presumably as a result of the civil war which began in that year. With the presidency of Mosquera in 1845 there began another interlude of peace conducive to literary production, and from then into the 1860's many newspapers appeared in Bogotá. One paper, *El Día*, managed the miracle of uninterrupted publication even in the early 1840's, largely through the determination of Bogotá's foremost printer, José Antonio Cualla.[1] Its continuous weekly appearance through 1851 gives it the record of longevity for its era. *El Día* was not primarily a literary paper, but *costumbrista* articles often appeared in it.

Other Bogotá periodicals which contributed significantly to the development of the *costumbrista* movement between 1840 and 1860 were *El Duende* (1846-1847), *El Neogranadino* (1848-1857), *El Pasatiempo* (1851-1854), *El Album* (1856-1857), and *La Biblioteca de Señoritas* (1858-1859). As their titles indicate, all these were essentially literary papers except *El Neogranadino*, in which most space was given to current events, political propaganda, and public affairs. Almost all the periodicals of the mid-century period, except those devoted exclusively to partisan political vituperation, published an occasional *cuadro de costumbres*.

With respect to *costumbrismo*, this prosperous era of literary journalism reached a climax with the founding of the weekly *El Mosaico* in December, 1858. The importance of this magazine and the writers who edited it and contributed to it makes possible and convenient, though slightly arbitrary, a division of the writers to be studied hereafter into two large groups—those who established themselves as *costumbristas* before the advent of *El Mosaico*, and those of a younger generation whose careers as writers on manners are more closely associated with that paper. Those who may be included among the pre-Mosaicos are José Caicedo Rojas, José Manuel Groot, Juan Francisco Ortiz, Rafael Eliseo Santander, Juan de Dios Restrepo (Emiro Kastos), and Medardo Rivas.

CAICEDO ROJAS

José Caicedo Rojas (1816-1897) was a *bogotano*, a representative to congress in 1852 (where he favored legislation to protect the Indian), director for a time of the Academia Colombiana, and a musician. As a writer, he has three unpublished plays, two historical novels, a volume of poetry, and

---

[1] Cualla was more than a printer; he was the authors' friend par excellence. His devotion to letters had an incalculable influence on the literature of mid-century Colombia. See Gustavo Otero Muñoz, *Historia del periodismo en Colombia* (Selección Samper Ortega de Literatura Colombiana, Vol. LXI; 3d ed.; Bogotá: Editorial Minerva, n.d.), pp. 64-65.

pamphlets on music, morals, and biography. He is best known for his *costumbrista* articles and historical anecdotes.

In 1846 and 1847 Caicedo was editor, with Domingo A. Maldonado, of the diminutive weekly *El Duende* (seventy-eight numbers), clearly inspired in Larra, though its masthead slogan was from Cervantes: "En cuerpos pequeños buscad grandeza de alma, nobleza de sentimientos y bondad de corazón." Most of Caicedo's *costumbrista* articles, many with the word *duende* in the title, were published in this paper.[2]

A collection of Caicedo Rojas' articles was published in 1883 under the title *Escritos escogidos*. The first section of the volume, "Apuntes de ranchería," contains some articles of *costumbrista* interest, though not many of them fully meet the requirements of the proper sketch. One of the most interesting is called "El tiple." The *tiple*, a simplification of the guitar, is the national musical instrument of Colombia. The article demonstrates the importance of this instrument, and the music produced with it, in the life of the *campesino*. Caicedo discusses the origin of music among primitive people, the Colombian national dances (*bambuco, torbellino,* and *caña*), and copies down some delightful folk *coplas*, which are always accompanied by the *tiple*. For example:

    Mi mujer y mi mulita
    Se me murieron a un tiempo;
    ¡Qué mujer, ni qué demonios!
    Mi mulita es lo que siento.

"El tiple," judging from the frequency of its reprinting, was the most popular of Caicedo's articles. The subject, indeed, is fascinating, but the style is undistinguished and at times even incorrect, and the author's attitude toward the *pueblo*, whose music he apparently esteems, is condescending and romantic. In spite of its formal, semi-scientific method, the article may be considered a *cuadro* of the descriptive type. It has value, too, as an early example of scholarly interest in Spanish-American folklore.

Another article in the collection, "Antiguo modo de viajar por la montaña del Quindío," ought to have been a *cuadro de costumbres*, but Caicedo gave it such a strange form that its purpose is entirely obscured. The article is inspired by a picture

---

[2] Through an unfortunate lapse (the author's own) in microphotography technique, this curious paper was not available for this study of Caicedo's work.

of the same title by the artist Ramón Torres Méndez, whose unique color drawings of realistic scenes from city and country life are highly informative and of great interest to the student of Andean manners. The picture shows a man, woman, and child being transported across the mountains of the Cordillera Central between Ibagué and Cartago in chairs bound to the backs of husky porters. The high spot of the piece, which is marred by triviality, digression, and insipid efforts at humor, is a satirical passage introduced by way of identifying the travellers in the picture.

A very good article called "Dos paseos al salto" is based on a custom important in Bogotá social life from the earliest colonial times to now—the excursion to famous Tequendama falls in the Bogotá river a few miles from the capital. The falls have a four-hundred-foot drop of such beauty and grandeur as to be worthy of the devotion the *bogotano* has for them. A tribute to them is inevitable in the repertory of every Bogotá poet, and they are hardly less important to the *costumbrista*.

Caicedo's article is dedicated to Eugenio Díaz, who wrote a sketch about the *ruana*, the Colombian poncho, and opens with a deserved eulogy of this magnificent garment.

> Este compañero generoso y *confortable*, que abriga, que protege, que consuela; este emblema de la vida dulce y tranquila, de la paz y quietud del cuerpo y del espíritu, merecería ser conocido, no sólo de los napolitanos, inventores del *dolce farniente*, sino de todos los pueblos donde se estime en algo la comodidad, el abrigo, la pereza, y todo lo que hay de sabroso y deleitable.

After a description of all the varieties of poncho known in Colombia, Caicedo continues with his own experience with the *ruana* on a trip to Tequendama with a group of friends. On the way out his horse bolted as he was putting the poncho over his head and he could not find the reins. "Llegué a creerme en las *siete cabrillas*, como si fuera en Clavileño, tal era la fuerza del viento que me combatía de frente." He was finally rescued by a stock-driver who pulled the *ruana* off his head as he flew by. After viewing the falls Caicedo suffered another accident, and the *ruana*—or lack of it—again was the cause of his embarrassment. In helping a lady over a difficult place in the path he put too great a strain on his fashionably tight trousers, and—"dar ella el salto . . . y sentir yo un estallido en la parte posterior de mi cuerpo, que bien claramente conocí lo que era, fué todo obra del momento." A long *ruana* of the *bayetón* type would have covered his embarrassment, but, alas, he was wearing a short, light one that scarcely reached his waist.

Caicedo refrains from describing the falls, and for a sound reason:

> Tuvimos los viajeros la satisfacción de ver el Salto, aunque ya lo sabíamos de memoria. ... Lo vimos ... lo oímos, lo palpamos, respiramos sus perfumes y sus nieblas, y. ... Pero qué diantre! ¿Me pondré yo a hacer ahora una descripción del Salto, cuando las hay por docenas, en prosa y en verso, más o menos dignas del asunto?

The account of the second trip to the falls is anticlimactic and irrelevant, as the author admits by tacking it on with the remark "ya que hoy estamos de aventuras y anécdotas," and is of little interest. If the second half is ignored, this article is a very successful *cuadro*. It presents excellent information about the *ruana* and a fashionable *paseo al salto*, and Caicedo's style in this case is clever, humorous, and, for the most part, clear and uninvolved.

Three Caicedo Rojas sketches appear in the Selección Samper Ortega de Literatura Colombiana, Volume XXII. They are "El tiple," already mentioned, "El Duende en un baile," and "Las criadas de Bogotá."

"El Duende en un baile" was written for Caicedo's paper, *El Duende,* in 1846. The first part of the article is done in verse, in *romance* and *redondilla* meters. A servant brings to the author a verbal invitation to Doña Pepa's dance, and the servant's unlettered language is cleverly accommodated to the meter:

> Que le *espachaba* a decir
> mi señora doña Juana
> que es su señor, que mañana
> tenga la bondad de ir,
> porque tiene una *riunión*:
> que es una cosa casera,
> y que sin falta lo espera
> al punto de la oración.

As he reaches Doña Pepa's house El Duende changes from verse to prose, because "los versos son malos colores para pintar, y deben hallarse pocas veces en la paleta del escritor de costumbres." (An early instance of an author's calling himself a *costumbrista*.) He enters, by a bad-smelling vestibule, a parlor arranged in bad taste—odd furniture from all over the house, flamboyant garlands painted on the walls, a bed with thick yellow columns like a Tuscan tomb visible through the bedroom door, three tallow candles in unmatched glass chimneys hanging from the beams of the ceiling. The ladies sit in rows against the walls (the men are congregated in the corridor outside), their solemn mein contrasting with their gaudy dress. El Duende comments on the virtues of simplicity in dress and adornment. At the end of each dance the women return to the wall and the men go to the middle of the room. Caicedo wonders that the men neither take seats with their partners nor seek their company between dances.

> Pero en estos bailes, no señor: se va por bailar, y nada más que por bailar . . . por el placer brutal de brincar, estropearse la figura y entrar en calor; no se va a buscar los placeres de la sociedad, los goces de la civilización; se va a beber brandy, se va a ostentar una educación poco culta y poco esmerada, y a hacer alarde de una ordinariez inaguantable.

The music is not very good either—"me cosieron a puñaladas aquellos malditos clarinetes y aquella infernal trompa." Failing to find a partner for the *contradanza*, El Duende sits down with one of the chaperons.

> Me instalé, pues, junto a mi mamá (es decir, no era mía) y tijeretazo por allí, tijeretazo por allá, nos dimos forma de pasar el rato, departiendo en sabrosa plática, haciendo corte de mangas a cada prójimo que pasaba por delante de nosotros. ¡Que lengua tan brava, Virgen Santísima!, yo mismo tenía miedo de aquella mamá, que donde clavaba la sin hueso levantaba ampolla.

After many another motive for disgust—one of them a duel over a girl's mistake in promising the same dance to two men—the author departs. The article ends with a philippic against the bad taste of such "social" functions, "adonde va tanto joven sin cultura, tanto viejo sin delicadeza." The reader wonders whether the author himself, *viejo* or not, is not a little lacking in *delicadeza*; there remains no doubt that El Duende is a snob!

"El Duende en un baile" is one of Caicedo's best *artículos de costumbres*. Development is logical and climactic, and digression is limited. His description is full and felicitous in expression, producing simultaneously realism and humor through likely figures and effective use of colloquialism, and the festive verse is first rate. The satire may be unfair, but it is good.

"Las criadas de Bogotá," an exercise in wit in the classification of servants, is less ambitious than the previous article, but imparts in an entertaining manner considerable information regarding the attitude of the served toward the servant.

The introduction is packed with puns, a kind of humor that tempted the average *costumbrista* satanically.

> Con el temor, pues, que naturalmente inspira una materia, de suyo y de ajeno tan delicada y seria, que tiene tantas espinas, tantas entradas y salidas, tanta servidumbre, y en fin, tantas muelas, como dice el vulgo, ponemos el pie, o mejor dicho, la mano, en el terreno, para hacer con mucha desconfianza alguna pálida descripción, aunque lo pálido no sea lo más común en el tipo que hemos elegido por hoy.

The selfless *criada antigua*, "fincas raíces que nacían, vivían y morían en el hogar doméstico de sus protectores, y apegadas a él como el bejuco a la encina," is now an almost extinct species. Modern servants are of four classes, designated by terms borrowed from grammar—*copulativas, disyuntivas, condicionales,* and *causales*. The first type has an air and polish acquired from close association with the upper classes.

> Ella se reputa como la subsecretaria, procuradora y delegataria; en una palabra el *fac totum de la cité* que dice el Barbero de Sevilla, y que yo agarro por los cabellos, y ensarto o inserto aquí, para que los aficionados no se quejen de falta de latines.

She can even talk about geography:

> Si se ofrece, habla de Europa, aunque *al oído*, como dicen los músicos, y agrega que el señorito . . . había escrito de *Animalia*, y que pasaría de *París a Francia* y de *Inglaterra a Londres* para embarcarse en *Tautánton* y que volvería por los Estados Unidos de *Nu Yor*.

The second type is *flotante*—she changes employers often and takes interest in nothing beyond collecting her pay and stealing as much as she can. She is the mainstay of the household labor force, goes barefooted, wears a plain mantilla during the week and on Sunday a panama hat with a bright ribbon, and speaks a strange, half-barbarous, stream-of-consciousness jargon. The *criadas condicionales* are engaged only temporarily to perform as kitchen helper, wet nurse, or nursemaid.

Caicedo forsakes charity altogether in describing the fourth class:

> Estas salen de la ínfima del pueblo, con perdón de la igualdad de la democracia, y son el *non plus ultra* de la mugre, desaseo y estupidez. . . . La cabeza, semejante a la de Medusa, causa espanto y horror; tal es su desgreño. Aquel enredo inexplicable de crines negras e indomables, sólo puede compararse a alguno de esos pleitos que en los juzgados y notarías dan ocupación y alimento a la larga familia de abogados, leguleyos, jueces, gendarmes y aficionados.

These poor creatures are essentially bearers, though they perform all the household tasks too humble for the rest of the hierarchy. The conclusion is digressive and abrupt, but the article is a good type sketch.

Though Caicedo cannot be appraised conclusively on the basis of the articles discussed here, it is clear that he is a competent writer of manners. In some of his sketches he falls rather short of success, but in "Dos paseos al salto," a first-rate familiar essay, "El Duende en un baile," effective satire in spite of its snobbishness, and even in "Las criadas de Bogotá," Caicedo shows that he understands the *costumbrista* genre and can use its varied forms with credit to himself and pleasure for his readers. His clear debt to Larra lends strength to the evidence that Colombian *costumbrismo* was the legitimate offspring of a Spanish parent.

GROOT

Another *costumbrista* writing in the mid-1840's was José Manuel Groot (1800-1878), a Colombian of Dutch ancestry who enjoyed some fame as a painter and wrote for an imposing number of periodicals, including *El Duende, El Mosaico,* and *El Día.* As a youth he was a Voltairian rationalist, but in 1849 and 1850 he was editor of *El Catolicismo,* a religious organ for which he wrote over two hundred articles. His most enduring work, still highly regarded, is his *Historia eclesiástica y civil de Nueva Granada* (1869).

Groot's *costumbrista* production seems to have been limited, but its quality was generally good. He is represented here by five articles in the Selección Samper Ortega, Volume XXI. The earliest of these articles, and one of his most popular, is a familiar epic originally published in three episodes entitled "Nos fuimos a Ubaque," "Nos quedamos en Chipaque," and "Llegamos a Ubaque." It is an amusing account of the hardships and hazards of a family vacation trip, the humor of which rests primarily on the misadventures and speech of the servants, the vanity of the young daughters in the family, and the embarrassment of everybody. The atmosphere and events are both realistic, and the article has considerable historical value. However, the piece is so long that its homely charm wears thin.

"La barbería" (1858), another personal essay, describes three barbershops of different social eras. The first belongs to the earliest revolutionary period, and it was there that the author and other Colombians patriotically left their Spanish *coletas* (hair queues).

> Este diablo de colgajo fastidioso caía sobre la espalda, y cuando uno volvía la cabeza para un lado u otro, le azotaba por el opuesto. La libertad de la coleta, que trajo consigo la del coleto, no se ha apuntado entre las conquistas con la revolución del 20 de julio, y yo por mi parte quiero remediar la omisión, bendiciendo la tijera libertadora del maestro Lechuga.

The second is a democratic establishment of the early independence in which the barber refuses to allow the author to occupy a chair just vacated by a countryman of the *sabana*.

> —No es bueno sentarse en asiento que otro ha calentado, porque no sabe uno qué humores pueden pegársele.
> —La preocupación es buena—le dije—pero yo no tengo recelo de las gentes del campo que son muy alentadas.
> —Eso era antes—me replicó—; pero ahora no hay que fiarse, porque los malos humores se han regado por todas partes, y no hay guayabas sin gusanos.

The third, briefly treated, belongs to a fashionable French hairdresser whom the author patronizes only at the insistence of the women in his family.

The latest of the five articles, written in 1871, is a rare example of real *costumbrismo* in the service of politics. Called "La junta vecinal," it deals with the refusal of a small town to accept a proposal of the liberal government to establish public schools with imported Protestant teachers. In demonstrating the arch-conservatism and rigid orthodoxy of the *campesino,* Groot presents a realistic gallery of colorful rural characters. The tone is light throughout, and the article is entertaining, but its propagandistic intent is unmistakable.

The two most interesting articles, and those of greatest documentary value, are "Costumbres de antaño" and "La tienda de don Antuco." The first, written in 1865, is a medley of reminiscences about the principal religious holidays of the author's childhood. A great deal of space is given to the *pesebres* (Nativity scenes) of the Christmas season. Many of them were set up by certain artisans, especially tailors, who, though recognized experts, were insensitive to the niceties of scale and chronology.

> Ellos empezaban por poner el portal, y después, siguiendo el hilo de la historia, disponían lo demás por un orden cronológico tan ajustado, que muchas veces, junto a la casa de Herodes, seguía una gruta con su ermitaño rezando el rosario ante el crucifijo; más allá se veía una venta de indios en *chirriadera* y un

capuchino bailando con los hábitos arremangados; después, los reyes magos, y luego un batallón de soldados vestidos a la francesa, y así otras mil cosas, sin cometer mayor anacronismo.

The merriment of the season included, on Christmas Eve, a great traffic of servants bearing *buñuelos* and *empanadas* from house to house, midnight mass, singing to the accompaniment of the *tiple,* and dancing. "¡Felices tiempos!" comments Groot. "¡Cuánto mejor era esto que estar embalando cartuchos y haciendo revoluciones!"

Easter was a time for fine dress, especially on Maundy Thursday when it was the custom to visit churches to view the altars especially decorated for the Host to be consumed on Good Friday.

> ¿Quién no sabe que todo bicho viviente sube un punto más de su ordinario en el jueves santo? Desde el opulento capitalista hasta el altozanero y el mendigo, en todos, el termómetro de la vestimenta sube algunos grados.

The excitement of Corpus Christi began when the *alcaldes* of the city assigned to the women figures to be dressed for the procession two or three weeks later. Illustrated Bibles were much in demand. The city provided costumes of monsters and giants for the lower classes and enlisted at least ten men to be the dragon. On the morning of Corpus great crowds swarmed out of the houses to view the *bosques* (floats or tableaux) and triumphal arches set up in the streets. Groot's description of the *bosques* suggests the *fallas* of the contemporary Valencian fiesta.

> En uno se representaba el escribano con gorro y anteojos, escribiendo en su mesita, sobre la cual hay un montón de autos, tintero y plumas, y un gallo desplumado con un letrero que dice: *litigante.* Al pie de la mesa está amarrado del pescuezo un gato que maúlla medio ahorcado, símbolo de los escribanos. Más allá, en la otra esquina, hay otro bosque en que se ve a un enfermo en su cama, y al médico junto, que le toma el pulso a una mochila de plata que está a la cabecera de la cama.

About nine o'clock bands of buffoons make their entrance, and, after a period of riotous nonsense, there is silence, the chant of the *pange lingua* is heard, and the procession passes by, a grave company followed by soldiers in full dress.

"Costumbres de antaño" is a remarkable relation of events and customs lovingly and joyously remembered. Narration and description are both suggestively done, and the details presented are, uncannily, precisely those of most interest to the modern reader.

"La tienda de don Antuco," an excellent evocative article dated 1856, describes one of the few remaining stores where *tertulianos* are welcome—"No se ve allí, como en todas las demás tiendas, un cartel diciendo en letras gordas: *La tertulia perjudica,* porque don Antuco gusta mucho de ella."³

Don Antuco sells boots, shoes, and slippers, and miscellaneous notions such as bells, basins, ribbon, rope, and inkwells, but he is careful not to let trade interfere with conversation, for which he has provided seats in the dark recesses by the leather-covered doors. The shelves of the store are old boxes, darkened by age; the floor is stone and the ceiling is supported by massive beams, from one of which hangs a stick supporting items of merchandise and the scales, the latter so badly out of adjustment that a compensatory fist-sized stone is needed. The counters are covered with leather slicked by the dirt and wear of years of trade. "Esta misteriosa guarida," says Groot, "que le pone a uno en otro mundo, inspira cierto recogimiento y sabrosura."

> ¡Oh, qué ratos tan sabrosos los que se pasan en la tienda de don Antuco! Y si es lloviendo, mejor, y más si es en hora de oficina y que pueda uno decir: "Es imposible salir de aquí: aquí tengo que estarme en tertulia sin faltar a mi obligación ni gravar mi conciencia, puesto que lloviendo no estoy obligado implícitamente a ir a la oficina; porque el mojarme me haría daño, y la propia conversación es precepto de ley natural que obliga en conciencia." ¡Oh! entonces se echa uno más para atrás en el asiento y dice: "Ojalá no escampe en toda la tarde"; enciende otro tabaco y sigue con el cuento.

A beautiful apology for the *tertulia*!

The article is concluded with a delightful conversation between Don Antuco and a rustic artisan peddling a pair of newly-made shoes.

> —¿Y por esto cuánto *pedís*?
>
> —*Ahi* me dará *sumercé* diez reales—contestó el otro, rascándose el cogote y con una medio risita en la cara.
>
> —¡Diez reales esto!
>
> —Si el material está sumamente caro. Para qué lo he de engañar a *sumercé*; a mí me salen costando un peso, fuera de mi trabajo.

---

³ At least two anonymous articles—both entitled "No se admite tertulia"—described stores whose proprietors were of a different mind from Don Antuco. (*El Correo*, March 19, 1840; *El Album*, December 15, 1856.)

—Pero, hombre, si yo no los vendo aquí más que a peso, ¿cómo te voy a dar diez reales?

Et cetera, until a bargain is finally made.

Groot's five *cuadros* are remarkably even in quality. His style is vigorous and imaginative, rich in colloquial idiom and regional vocabulary (*ringlete, regodiento, ranga, alentado*, etc.), unmarred by self-conscious allusion or strained niceness. His greatest skill is in description, but his narration is passable, and his dialogue realistic. Also, his ability to evoke atmosphere is conspicuously superior, especially in "Costumbres de antaño" and "La tienda de don Antuco." And his greatest weakness is related to his evocative power—he is not content to evoke the past but insists, perhaps correctly, surely monotonously, on its superiority to the present.

Groot is strictly a writer of *cuadros*—not *artículos*—his "La junta vecinal" notwithstanding, for he is little interested in criticism or satire and, except for an occasional sarcastic aside, his characters and institutions are presented without exaggeration and without malice. He is an accurate recorder of manners who observed his fellows and his times with a keen and kindly eye.

ORTIZ

Juan Francisco Ortiz (1808-1875) was a member of the Mosaico circle and published an article in the first number of the periodical published by that group, but he had already been a practicing *costumbrista* for many years. Ortiz was born in Bogotá but was taken to the provinces as a child when his father was exiled for his part in the early independence movement. He returned to the capital when the Liberator Bolívar, grateful for the elder Ortiz' patriotic service, arranged a scholarship in the Colegio de San Bartolomé, from which Ortiz emerged a lawyer. He travelled widely within Colombia and visited Perú shortly before his death. Ortiz held many minor government offices, served as governor of Neiva and Pamplona provinces, and was prominent as a teacher and educator in Bogotá and Boyacá.

Ortiz was a prolific journalist, contributing to *El Neogranadino, La Guirnalda, El Porvenir,* and *El Mosaico,* and edited in 1848 a one-man paper called *El Tío Santiago,* the title of which he later used as a pseudonym. Otero Muñoz[4] credits him with one of the earliest Colombian attempts at the novel—*El oidor de Santafé*, or *El oidor Cortés de Mesa*, published in 1845—calls him a pioneer in writing travel literature, and says that he was noted for his humor and sarcasm. Other works are an epistolary novel called *Carolina la bella* and a posthumous volume of memoirs. According to Otero Muñoz, Ortiz probably wrote more *costumbrista* pieces than any other Colombian, but he is modestly represented in this study by four articles from the Selección Samper Ortega (Volume XXII), a collection called *Museo de cuadros de costumbres*, published in 1866 by the editors of *El Mosaico*, and a miscellany edited by Nepomuceno J. Navarro and José David Guarín under the title *Lirios y azucenas* (Socorro, 1871).

Ortiz' best known article is "Una taza de chocolate," a sentimental tribute to this symbol of all that is wholesome and cherished in Colombian social tradition. The article, which first appeared in *El Neogranadino* (December 30, 1848), consists of recollections (the first one dated before the author's birth!) of people and events pleasantly associated in the writer's memory with the drinking of chocolate—the house of a canon from which he watched the Viceroy and his retinue pass by in promenade in 1801, the house of his aunt in Tunja and a girl whose "ojos picarísimos mantenían con los míos un diálogo continuado," a journalist friend with whom he spent many evenings in literary conversation, and the sick room of a vivacious and gracious young girl to whom the author was devoted. It is a naively charming *cuadro*, presented with quiet humor and infectious nostalgia.

"Motivo por el cual," another of Ortiz' well-known pieces, is completely different—a familiar essay whose only purpose is to be humorous. In it Ortiz ostensibly presents his alibi for his bachelorhood, recounting how one rented horse that was too fast and another that was too slow frustrated his attempts to woo a *serrana* whom he had selected to be his wife. The humor derives from the incongruity of the author's burlesque passions and frustrations and a deliberate use of grotesque words. It is successful farce, and probably responsible for Ortiz' reputation as a humorist, but only slightly *costumbrista*.

---

[4] *Resumen de historia de la literatura colombiana* (4th ed.; Bogotá: Librería Voluntad, 1943), p. 231.

The article is perhaps most interesting as a late descendent of the line of burlesque *serranillas* fathered by the archpriest Juan Ruiz.

Another, but less successful, attempt at farce is "La serenata" (*El Neogranadino*, December 14, 1849), an account of an abortive serenade which ends with the honored lady's father setting his dogs on the serenaders. The description of the serenade proper is interesting, but too many unfunny digressions spoil the piece.

"El viaje de Don Pascualito" (in *Lirios y azucenas*) has much greater value both as literature and as *costumbrismo*. In it Ortiz presents a village bumpkin in whom a passionate desire to visit Paris was kindled by the tales, heard in the local billiard parlor, of an itinerant Picard who himself had never seen the city. Like many a tourist, Pascualito was most intrigued and attracted by the fleshier aspects of Parisian life. When an inheritance allowed Pascualito to reach Paris he quickly found a charming *grisette* to share his bed and board, but his idyll was shattered when the mistress took "French leave" with all of his funds. Only temporarily dismayed, Pascualito borrowed money, bought a fabulous wardrobe, and returned to Colombia. On the way home he conceived the monstrous hoax of representing himself as a learned and practiced physician, confident that his fine clothes and airs would insure him against incredulity. And he was right. Pascualito, the author says, now enjoys professional and social esteem, is about to marry an heiress, and aspires to a cabinet post. "¡Cuántos de nuestros compatriotas habrán hecho el viaje de Don Pascualito! ¡Y qué exacto es el dicho del poeta latino! 'Coelum non animum mutant qui trans mare currunt.'"

Some of Ortiz' criticism in this *artículo* is naive and trivial— he sees the billiard parlor as a seat of corruption, and immoral women, who are not found *only* in Paris, as a threat to respectable social institutions—but he is effective in his attack on the conditions of academic decadence and public credulity which have brought the practice of medicine to a sordid state.

> Así fué que entonces se vieron doctorcitos flamantes que no sabían sumar; doctorcitos muy almidonados y peripuestos que no podían traducir una página de latín; mediquillos de a ciento en carga que no habían saludado la terapéutica; pequeños Esculapios que ignoraban de todo punto la anatomía, y pensaban que Linneo había sido un español del tiempo de la conquista; hombrecitos sin

corazón, para quienes la salud del género humano era un juego, y que miraban la más grande, la más respetable de todas las profesiones como una vil especulación.

Above all, Ortiz means to criticize the tendency of his compatriots to idolize any miserable fool who has spent a few months abroad and has returned with clothing of the latest cut and the ability to garble a few words of French. This is a common theme in *costumbrismo* and one which both Mesonero and Larra had used—a change of clime does not change a fool.

This article, like "La serenata," is digressive, but here the author's wanderings are an asset; each one offers a rewarding metaphor, an outburst of sarcasm or satire, or an especially humorous quality. The narrative has a point and a good one, the character of Don Pascualito is handled with good effect, and the humor is varied—dry, subtle, whimsical, incisive. The style is sometimes cumbersome but is in general piquant and imaginative.

The articles discussed above show Ortiz in three lights. In the first he is a *cuadrista*, a philosopher of the armchair; in the second he is purely an entertainer, writing comedy for its own sake; and in "El viaje de Don Pascualito" he is satirist and critic. In these three aspects he is representative of Colombian *costumbrismo*, and, as a prolific writer of essays, he may have influenced the formation of the genre in these three molds. He was reasonably successful in all three forms. He is not a stylist, but he does have skill in humorous writing. He makes good use of grotesque colloquial vocabulary and has a curiously effective technique of creating elaborate puns by applying a familiar expression to a bizarre situation.

SANTANDER

Rafael Eliseo Santander (1809-1883), though his articles are dubious of classification and quality, must be dealt with here because Colombians consider him a reputable *costumbrista*—his works appear in the Selección Samper Ortega (Volume XXII) and in the *Museo de cuadros de costumbres*—and because he had a hand in the founding of the Mosaico.

Santander was a lawyer who served in the congress, as secretary to the supreme court, and held other administrative and judicial positions. He co-edited, with José Caicedo Rojas and José María Samper, a weekly called *El Trovador*, of which thirteen numbers appeared in 1850, and he contributed to *El Duende*, *El Neogranadino*, and *El Tiempo*.

"Los artesanos" is apparently one of Santander's earliest articles, published originally in *El Duende*. His purpose, presumably, is to compare the artisan of colonial days with his post-independence counterpart to the advantage of the latter, since he announces himself the champion of the working man. The conclusion shows the patronizing attitude which pervades the article and renders suspect the author's protestations of enlightened liberalism:

> Sólo deseamos que nuestros artesanos sean piadosos, creyentes sinceros, sin fanatismo ni hipocresía; que se ilustren sin alcanzar a entrever el impiísmo, que todo lo pervierte; y que sean tan exigentes como quieran en cuanto por derecho les toque, mas sin propasarse con groseras vulgaridades, con inepcias de taberna, ni con manejos soeces. Para nada de esto, aquí concluimos, jurando no proceder con malicia, etc.

This concluding sentence, or fraction of a sentence, is a good example of the ineptness of style which makes almost inextricable whatever valid appreciation of working-class life the article may contain. The confusion is insurmountable.

In "Las fiestas en mi parroquia," written a year or two later, Santander again sets the old against the new, this time with more success. He represents himself as a man of sixty-five (he was thirty-nine) to lend authority to his eulogy of a forgotten era. He sets out on a bright July morning for the *fiestas*, his heart gay in anticipation and his mind full of recollections of youth, and, after a good description of the preparation of the *plaza* for the bullfighting of the afternoon, becomes involved in an argument with a brash nephew over the comparative merits of his and the nephew's eras. His opinion is violent:

> La gravedad y gentileza, la decencia y compostura, el lujo y magnificencia que reinaban en aquellos buenos tiempos, ¿qué se han hecho? Ruido y desorden, desvergüenza y osadía, oropeles y zarandajas de ningún valor, es sólo lo que veo, porque lo positivo todo ha desaparecido.

The bootless argument continues until the *fiesta* concludes unexpectedly with the escape of a bull and the collapse of the spectators' platform.

> Y yo, molido y escarmentado, huí de la plaza para nunca volver a toros, prefiriendo molestar a mis lectores con cuadros tan pálidos como éste que aquí finaliza.

This article is better composed and infinitely more entertaining than "Los artesanos," but even so the reader is inclined to agree that it is pale. The thesis of the piece is of no interest and its value as pure description is easily surpassed by other articles in the Colombian repertory on the same subject.

"La Nochebuena" is disappointing in that it barely touches on the practices and ceremonies of Christmas, using them only as a setting for devoutly idealistic reflections on the significance of the holiday. Santander returns here to his obsessive skepticism about contemporary manners but concludes that even the decadent modern may be sincere in his enthusiasm for the celebration of the Nativity.

One of Santander's most praised articles is "El raizalismo vindicado," written in reply to imputations of *raizalismo* made by Juan de Dios Restrepo. Its purpose is to demonstrate that *raizalismo*, which he defines as "un profundo amor, un amor sin término al pedacito de tierra en que a la Providencia le vino en voluntad mandarnos crecer y multiplicarnos," is not a decadent state of mind. It is doubtful that Santander convinced Restrepo, a true cosmopolitan and liberal. The article has humor and charm, but little *costumbrista* value.

"La Calle Honda" and "Historia de unas viruelas," the latter Santander's acknowledged masterpiece, both belong to history or the historical anecdote, not to *costumbrismo*.

One must conclude that Santander contributed little to the development of the *cuadro de costumbres*.

RESTREPO

Juan de Dios Restrepo (1823-1894) stands apart from his contemporary *costumbristas* in many ways. He was born and lived most of his life in Antioquia, though he occasionally made long visits to Bogotá; all of his writing was done during a ten-year period in his youth; he is not known to have published poetry; he displays, for his time, exceedingly wide culture and enlightenment; and he was an unusually penetrating social critic.

Most of his literary efforts—short articles on manners, economics, history, and travel—appeared in *El Pueblo*, of Medellín, and *El Neogranadino* and *El Tiempo*, of Bogotá, between 1850 and 1860. About 1860 Restrepo seems to have stopped writing altogether to devote his energies to agriculture and mining. His articles have been collected in two editions of almost identical content.[5] His pseudonym, Emiro Kastos, is better known than his legal name.

Unfortunately for the student of *costumbrismo*, not all of Restrepo's articles on manners, most of them excellent, can be classified as *artículos* or *cuadros de costumbres*; they are often purely expository or argumentative and their manner is too intense, too formal. For example, a group of six articles on the position of woman in society and her defenselessness before the customs of courtship and marriage yields only two which can logically be discussed here. The earliest of these is "Coquetería," which appeared in *El Neogranadino* on January 31, 1851.

The coquetry of Bogotá women was a favorite topic of mid-century moralists, and the periodicals of the time printed many outcries against it. Restrepo's article is not one of his best, but it is interesting for its rather revolutionary attitude toward flirtatious women. Restrepo's coquette is a charming, reflective woman who had loved and been deceived at the age of seventeen and, finding thereafter no object for true affection, had resorted to coquetry as the only means of preserving dignity in a superficial society. The cause of her pathetic state—and Restrepo returns repeatedly to this theme—is "la educación frívola i descuidada que se nos da." Restrepo seems to hold that her coquetry is justified as her only revenge against a male-dominated society. He further allows, with a touch of irony, that a considerable talent is involved:

> En efecto, cuánto tino no es menester para flotar como la espuma sin sumerjirse sobre el océano de las pasiones humanas; cuánto talento para hacer promesas que no sean enteramente promesas, para prodigar sonrisas que sean algo mas que amabilidad i algo ménos que amor, para ponerse enfrente de todos los deseos como la esperanza, i huir cuando se la crea tener entre las manos como la felicidad!

This is direct talk for Colombia in 1851, but Restrepo goes even further with the view that coquetry is not only a solace to woman but a boon to society in general:

> Sea lo que fuere, la coquetería es en cuestiones de amor lo que la urbanidad en asuntos de sociedad. I así como las atenciones i las palabras de amistad que nos prodigamos recíprocamente no en-

---

[5] Emiro Kastos, *Colección de artículos escogidos* (Bogotá: Imprenta de Pizano y Pérez, 1859); *Artículos escogidos de Emiro Kastos* (London: J. M. Fonnegra, 1885); also, Volume XXIX of the Selección Samper Ortega is devoted to Restrepo.

> gañan sino a los necios, las sonrisas agasajadoras de las coquetas
> solo se les convierten en sustancia a los inespertos o a los tontos.
> Sin embargo, suprímase la urbanidad con sus respetos convencio-
> nales, con sus palabras almibaradas i la sociedad se vuelve ina-
> guantable: exclúyanse de los bailes i de las tertulias a las co-
> quetas, que tienen para todo el mundo alguna palabra afectuosa,
> alguna sonrisa acariciadora, i entónces, no quedando en circulacion
> sino los afectos verdaderos—guarismo de pocas cifras—las re-
> uniones perderian su atractivo i animacion, i mas de cuatro que,
> en materia de afectos, a falta de realidad nos gusta la ficcion, nos
> quedariamos a buenas noches.

This is an enlightened and fair-minded statement, and it puts Restrepo at least half a century ahead of his time in social criticism. Clearly, Restrepo is no respecter of convention for its own sake.

Artistically "Coquetería" does not stand close scrutiny. Although it is written with humor and force, it is too long and in the narrative part strays too far from the subject. The conclusion is a masterpiece of irrelevance disastrous to the artistic effect of the article.

Lest it be concluded from his reasoned views on coquetry that Restrepo was always above and immune to the conventions of his time, a look at his attitude toward reading is appropriate. In "Vanidad i desengaño" (*El Tiempo*, June 15, 1858) Restrepo presents a young lady who was corrupted, because of insufficient education, to be sure, by reading novels, mostly French.

> Amen de que las novelas hacen perder el gusto por los estudios
> positivos i las ocupaciones sérias, enferman la imajinacion, falsean
> el carácter i lanzan el alma en aspiraciones fantásticas. . . . La
> novela francesa, sobre todo, que arroja impúdica al lector des-
> nudos sus personajes i sus pasiones, es tósigo mortal para una
> adolescente.

But another girl was saved because her "alma recta, sencilla i honrada" led her to prefer Scott and Richardson!

The last of these six articles is artistically the best. Called "Una botella de brandi i otra de jinebra" (*El Tiempo*, August 23, 1859), its theme is similar to that in "Vanidad i desengaño" and others—a marriage ruined by the vanity and extravagance of woman—but this time the point of view is male.

An old school friend of the author, an intelligent but simple man named Telésforo Cascajón, tells the story of his brief marriage, at his mother's insistence, to the beautiful and gracious Sofía. During the courtship Sofía endorsed and encouraged Telésforo's simple tastes, but, once married, she plunged him into an orgy of extravagance which drove him to return her and her dowry to her father. Telésforo had been completely deceived by the extravagant coquette and his heart was bitterly broken. As he tells his story to the author he drinks frequently and impartially from bottles of gin and brandy—hence the title of the article—and at the end of the story and the bottles the author puts him to bed.

The introduction is curious and a little irrelevant. The author had had a dream in which he was carried by a little devil, who might well be called Asmodeo, he says, to see a grotesque representation of society—a chicken yard in which each fowl persecuted every bird weaker and smaller than he. That depressing dream, added to the coldness of the day, left him in no mood for an early morning caller, but he received Telésforo gladly, he says, because "los amigos de colejio tienen el mismo privilejio que el hijo pródigo."

This article is richer in style than any of the others on the same subject, and it more exactly fills the requirements of *costumbrismo* in that it abandons the tone of preachment dominant in some of the others and relies on example and ironic humor for its didactic effect. It is written with imagination and has incisive figures and acute satirical asides. In the conclusion, incidentally, Restrepo gives further evidence of his typical rationality and tolerance. After he has put Telésforo to bed, he observes:

> A muchos, que se lanzan en el juego o la embriaguez para aturdirse, la multitud poco reflexiva los llama con desprecio *corrompidos,* cuando para el filósofo observador son únicamente *desgraciados.*

In Restrepo's articles on marriage and woman's attitude toward it there seems to be a change of opinion as the author becomes older. In the earliest articles he shows a realistic appreciation of the dilemma of woman in a society in which marriage is an absolute requirement for a normal life, and he seems to sympathize with her, even to the extent of justifying the coquetry with which she fights back. In the later articles his sympathy shifts somewhat and he comes closer to the conventional view that feminine frivolity and extravagance are the major cause of unhappy marriages, still maintaining, however, that these faults of feminine character are the product of a defective environment. In all of the articles he holds firm to the opinion that a more solid education for women would solve most of their problems.

In another group of six articles Restrepo turns to analysis and criticism of Colombian society in more general terms—materialism, sloth, hypocrisy—and again his manner is not usually that of the pure *costumbrista*. The earliest of the articles, "Pobre i rico" (*El Tiempo*, April 10, 1855), can, however, be considered an *artículo de costumbres* because of the epistolary narrative device on which it rests.

"Pobre i rico" deals with the materialism which has come to be the sole motive and exclusive criterion in all human relations, and, although Restrepo localizes the problem, his introduction gives it a universal setting. He admits that modern materialism has benefited civilization but deplores its effect on the individual. He laments the disappearance of such disinterested passions as "la fe poderosa i profunda que hizo a la Europa precipitarse sobre el Asia" in the age of the Crusades and observes that now only a rich nation can be a great nation.

There follows a sharply ironic letter, supposedly written to the author by a young man named Horacio, an intelligent youth equipped to practice law, who found all doors closed to him by his extreme poverty. After several years of unbroken disillusionment he considered suicide but rejected it for a unique reason. The ancients, he says, took their own lives for love, to foil tyranny, or for other noble reasons, but "el suicidio por falta de dinero i de gozes es una vulgaridad de nuestros tiempos, invencion del materialismo moderno." One day a rich relative paid Horacio a gold *onza* for writing a love letter and, for reasons Horacio himself did not understand, he went to a gambling house and ran it into a small fortune. He bought a horse, a watch, and fashionable clothing and promptly became a new man, with friends and opportunities in abundance. Having "arrived" socially, Horacio had to find a profession. The choice was obvious, but the decision was difficult.

> Queriendo adoptar una profesion lucrativa observé que, en nuestras ciudades llamadas mercantiles, las industrias que crian valores, los negocios de mútuas conveniencias en que todos ganan, no existen; ellas son un palenque, en que los diestros se ocupan en la evanjélica tarea de despojar a los necios, donde los pocos que tienen dinero esplotan las dificultades, las angustias de los que no lo tienen; donde la usura egoista, exajerada, implacable, la usura que no corre continjencias, no piensa, no trabaja, pero gana siempre, es la única industria popular, la sola especulacion fruc-

tuosa. Antes de dar el primer paso en esas operaciones innobles, me detuve como César ántes de pasar el Rubicon; pero al fin mis buenos instintos sucumbieron, i sin compasion ni escrúpulos de ninguna clase, abrí una de esas pequeñas oficinas de ájio a las cuales no ha habido todavía quien tenga la franqueza de poner por rótulo en la puerta: Aquí se esplotan las miserias del prójimo.

Horacio prospers financially and socially in his new venture and concludes that "la riqueza, de cualquier modo que se adquiera, es la absolucion de todos los pecados."

The article is a bitter indictment, which the author tempers with a concluding statement that wealth as the product of work, intelligence, and courage is a legitimate force and an unquestioned distinction. Although Restrepo exaggerates, as the satirist often must, his observation is sound and his criticism just, as a study of Colombian economics will amply demonstrate.

The latest article of this group is the most brilliant, but it is not *costumbrismo*. Called "Enfermedades sociales" (*El Tiempo*, November 29, 1859), it is a searching examination into the evils which impede Colombian progress and democracy. It eloquently reveals the enlightenment and understanding which qualify Restrepo as a social critic.

Three of Restrepo's articles, made up of brief satirical sketches of social types, seem to have been patterned after the Larra article called "Varios caracteres," in which Larra flays the individuals that come to his attention as he sits idly in a café. The first of these, "Una noche en Bogotá," appeared in *El Pasatiempo* on April 10, 1852. After a rather lyric introduction the author deplores, with all his customary acerbity, "que en esta Aténas del Sur-América no encuentra, siquiera el domingo por la noche, un ciudadano honrado donde pasar dos horas en solaz i divertimiento," and then recounts a visit to an exhibition of "estatuas."[6] But the author is more interested in the audience than in the performance; he satirizes briefly the miser to whom waste is so abhorrent that he eats used mustard plasters, an ostensibly virtuous girl who is at that moment arranging a clandestine meeting with a soldier, a parasitic dandy, a pompous amateur politician, and a girl whose novelistic concept of romance leads her to seek a Saracen for a husband.

---

[6] These "estatuas" are apparently the same "cuadros mimoplásticos" of which Guarín writes—a series of symbolical or historical tableaux presented to a paying audience. This curious form of public diversion would seem to deserve more than the brief and ambiguous treatment it receives from Restrepo and Guarín.

"Arturo i sus habladurías" (*El Pueblo*, February 8, 1856) employs the same technique but shifts the scene to Medellín. The author's informant is Arturo, "joven de imajinacion traviesa i picaresca," and the occasion is a Sunday *paseo*. The characters who receive critical treatment are a girl who depends too heavily on cosmetics, women who are incapable of social conversation, a hypocritical usurer ("un famoso bandido que va a morir en olor de santidad"), a ridiculous fifty-year-old dandy, and an innocent maid victimized by malicious gossip.

"Mosaico" (*El Tiempo*, July 6, 1858) has no framework at all, beginning *in medias res* with a listing of social types carefully characterized and neatly labeled. The first in the *pepita jamona*, a spinster of forty who acts like a girl of eighteen, but "con todas sus pretensiones de inocencia i de virjinidad de corazon, esta liebre corrida tiene mas recámaras que un laberinto." Her male counterpart is the *pepito emancipado*, the bachelor dandy who at forty-five decides he wants a wife, not realizing in his vanity that he is no longer "moneda apetecida i circulante" in the marriage mart. Many of these ultimately "atrapan por ahí cualquiera Maritornes espantable, o echan anclas en una viuda descreída, o se estrellan contra los ángulos salientes de alguna cuarentona fosilizada."

The *joven juicioso* is judicious and well behaved because he lacks the talent, originality, and imagination to be otherwise. This innocuous mediocrity is much esteemed by society and those who have it "viven considerados i mueren ricos." The *hombre grave*, dressed in black, silent and rigid as a caryatid, respected for his austerity, is losing favor because "se ha descubierto que nada hai en la creacion tan circunspecto, tan silencioso, tan solemne i tan grave como un jumento."

A large class which Restrepo calls the *sonámbulos* includes the "distraídos, desmañados, crédulos, incapazes o necios" like the man who expects to reform the frivolous girl he marries, the man who loses his fortune and wonders why he loses his friends, and those who think that Colombia has a great future because she has seaports, raw materials, and the isthmus of Panama.

> I nosotros que sin remuneracion, sin objeto, sin pretensiones, sin ambicion de ninguna clase, nos encargamos de fiscalizar la sociedad, arriesgándonos a que nos estropeen el bulto i nos midan las costillas, ¿qué otra cosa somos sino sonámbulos rematados?

"Mosaico" is clearly the best of the three articles, principally because it shows evidence of plan and thought which give it more unity than the others in spite of its lack of framework. Also, instead of mere surface sarcasm, which is the forte of the first two articles, "Mosaico" shows the discernment and penetration of valid social criticism. The conclusion of the article comes as close to pure levity as the stern Restrepo ever gets.

Two more Restrepo articles fall clearly into the *costumbrista* genre. One is a sprightly *artículo* and the other a masterful *cuadro*. The first, "Los pepitos" (*El Tiempo*, May 25, 1858), is Restrepo's only sketch in the conventional personal essay form. The *pepito* is a teen-aged boy whose obnoxious ubiquity is a threat to urbane society. Restrepo is careful to distinguish between this creature and that stalwart of Colombian society, the *cachaco*.

> El cachaco ha sido siempre el representante mas caracterizado del buen humor i del espíritu bogotanos. . . . Pero ¡oh frajilidad de las cosas humanas! este tipo orijinal, grandioso, elegante, oposicionista, este cuarto poder constitucional . . . este dictador de los salones, príncipe de la moda, rei de la crítica, el cachaco, en fin, ha sido absorbido, derrocado, eclipsado i amilanado por el *pepito*: el pepito es dueño de la situacion.

The *pepito* affects romantic disillusion and satiety, worships Byron, wears the latest French fashions, and holds that the ideal woman is one who has read the Encyclopedia and does not believe in anything. Restrepo finds him underfoot everywhere. In *tertulias* the *pepitos* monopolize conversation, citing Lamartine, Hugo, and Méry, and declaring that Boileau was a poor devil and Aristotle a simpleton; at dances they are dynamos of romance:

> Por todas partes estaban citando a las mujeres, haciéndoles señas, hablándoles al oído, revoloteando como mariposas. Por fortuna estos dorados querubines no se incendian sino en las llamas azules del amor platónico: entre ellos son raros los Lovelace i los Don Juan: el platonismo, primero que por el filósofo griego, fué inventado por algun pepito antediluviano.

"Los pepitos" is one of Restrepo's best articles, not only for its excellent delineation of a type, but because its good humor is a pleasant relief from the tone of aggravated cynicism which pervades most of his work.

The article for which Restrepo is best known, a *cuadro* called "Mi compadre Facundo" (*El Tiempo*, July 17, 1855), is a character study of a self-made man in the province of Antioquia. Facundo at twenty set out with his meager savings on a career of barter in the mining settlements. By dint of great economy and shrewd dealing he put together in six years a considerable capital, but he was waylaid on the road and robbed of it all—"quedó limpio como bolsillo de poeta español o de literato granadino." He began to rebuild his fortune with pick and shovel in the mines, later became a seeker of gold in Indian graves, a farmer, and ultimately a storekeeper. His business prospered, he acquired land, not always by ethical means, and became the most important man in town, the *gamonal*.

Such men as Facundo, who are not rare in rural Antioquia, says Restrepo, are admirable for their fortitude when poor, but, once wealthy, their continued practice of the sordid economies of their poverty makes them ridiculous. Facundo lives in a large house furnished with hard benches and stools—"al entrar en una de esas casas piensa uno involuntariamente en la otra vida." The family routine is reduced to hard work by day and prayer by night. Facundo's stolid, ugly, barefoot wife, whom he married for her energy and industry, works incessantly, as do his pretty daughters, also barefoot. The cuisine is as bare as the house—corn bread and vegetables, with meat occasionally, fowl almost never, and sugar an item of pure luxury—except when a rare guest occasions the "bodas de Camacho" demanded by Antioquian hospitality.

But this austere and wholesome regime is now threatened. Facundo foolishly sent his son to Bogotá to study law and he has returned with ideas of life and politics which frighten Facundo half to death.

> Lo mandé a que aprendiera a hacer escritos, i no sabe poner "ante usted parezco i digo." Pero ha venido con la cabeza llena de cucarachas i de grandezas. Dice que la casa está fea, como si yo no hubiera vivido en ella treinta años sin darme un dolor de cabeza: la comida siempre le parece mala, i la sala oscura cuando de noche se enciende una sola vela. ¡Obispo tenemos! Bonito estoi yo para hacer una boda todos los dias, i un velorio todas las noches! I esas mocozuelas de sus hermanas, a su ejemplo, andan ya todas *ideáticas* pidiendo galanuras, maestros de francés i otras cabronadas. Ya no quieren hacer nada, sino amansar tarima i chirriar zapatos. Dale con la *tuntunita* de aprender. ¡Dios me guarde de mujeres sabidas!

This outburst, with which Restrepo concludes the sketch, is an eloquent revelation of Facundo's character.

Restrepo in this article exhibits to excellent advantage his capacities for observation, understanding, and analysis of individuals and manners. The portrait of Facundo is vividly real.

There is some emphasis on the picturesque aspects of his character, but he is not idealized, nor is he merely quaint, and, although his personality dominates the *cuadro*, he is not presented only for his own sake but as a means to understanding the society he represents. The entire picture—Facundo, family, environment—is painted with impartiality, showing in equal light those aspects of Antioquian character the author deplores and those of which he is proud. For color, for discriminate use of detail, for depth of understanding, and for artistic unity, "Mi compadre Facundo" is a masterpiece of the *cuadro* in Colombia. Few articles can match it in general excellence.

In appraising Restrepo's work generally it is difficult to avoid superlatives. The earnestness, and the artistry as well, with which he exposes and condemns the idle, the frivolous, the pretentious, the hypocritical, the unjust, and the despotic in his society makes him almost unique among Colombian *costumbristas*, most of whom were generally content to paint quaint pictures and write an occasional personal essay of diffident satire on a minor foible of polite society. His vigorous satire stands in bold relief.

Restrepo also stands out for the breadth of his culture. He demonstrates a real familiarity with the literature of antiquity, Spain, France, and England, and a more than superficial knowledge of history and economics; and, further, his work shows the understanding, tolerance, and sense of justice that ought to be engendered, but often is not, by such wide cultural experience. He is free of prejudice and illusion and writes as a democrat and a realist. These factors qualify him eminently as a critic of society and even afford him a distinction of originality in a society fettered by sham and tradition and greatly in need of enlightened liberal influence.

The dominant characteristic of Restrepo's style is its strength and vigor. His language is not always correct, but it is never dull or rhetorical. His sentences are typically short, he almost invariably achieves clarity and concision, often even brilliance, and he has the epigrammatic quality which is a mark of the true essayist (on charity: "los hombres entienden la fraternidad un poco a la manera de Caín"; on resignation: "triste virtud inventada por el cristianismo para el uso especial de las mujeres").

It is a little difficult to fit Restrepo into the *costumbrista* classification, partly because few of his articles, even those dealing with manners, readily meet the requirements of the genre, partly because most of his work is marked by a critical intensity and an almost misanthropic cynicism which is inappropriate to *costumbrismo* unless it be relieved by humor, and humor is rare in Restrepo. However, if he is short on humor, he is rich in wit, sarcasm, satire, and a general grace which entertain the reader even if they do not amuse him, and those qualities, at least in his less formal articles, seem sufficient to satisfy the requirements of the sketch of manners. If it were not possible to consider part of Restrepo's work *costumbrismo*, the genre would lose one of its most brilliant Colombian practitioners.

Gustavo Otero Muñoz says that Larra was Restrepo's favorite author and that he consciously imitated the Spaniard in both form and substance.[7] The two men were certainly alike in their uncompromising attitude toward manners and ideas detrimental to progress and prosperity, and both are free from chauvinism in any form, which was not true of most *costumbristas*, Spanish or Colombian. In the matter of pessimism there is little to choose between them, for neither leans very far in the direction of good cheer. Restrepo's basic technique is like Larra's and even his style has the same economy, concision, and incisiveness. His greatest shortcoming in comparison with Larra is that he lacks the light touch which makes Larra's most cutting prose palatable—Restrepo's heavy hand too often molds a pill of criticism too large to swallow. However, in the absence of a better candidate, Restrepo probably deserves to be called "the Colombian Larra."

RIVAS

Medardo Rivas (1825-1901), who is probably Restrepo's nearest rival for the "Colombian Larra" title, is in a sense the forgotten man of Colombian *costumbrismo*. Isidoro Laverde Amaya, writing in 1890, notes that Rivas "es poco conocido y aplaudido en el mundo literario de Colombia,"[8] and, although he is represented by an article or two in some of the early anthologies of *costumbrismo*, he does not appear in the Selección Samper Ortega, the only presently accessible collection. He is mentioned in most manuals of literature but he is seldom placed in the first

---

[7] *Resumen de historia de la literatura colombiana*, p. 153.
[8] *Fisonomías literarias de Colombia* (Curaçao: Bethencourt e Hijos, 1890), p. 221.

rank of *costumbristas*. He deserves more attention than he has received.

Rivas had a varied career as writer, editor, publisher, planter, educator, and business man, and he travelled widely in Europe. As a youth he was an enthusiastic romantic. He wrote articles of manners, short stories, plays, philosophical treatises, and travel accounts, and had a part in the editorship of *La Revista Colombia, El Liberal,* and *El Siglo*. There is a one-volume collection of his works, published in Bogotá in 1883.

The most interesting part of Rivas' *costumbrista* production is a series of satirical portraits of imaginary characters, a gallery of Bogotá types, several of which appeared unsigned in *El Neogranadino* in 1852. The earliest of these (September 17) is "Emilio el doctor." Emilio is an over-educated young man who spends most of his time dodging debtors and complaining of his penury. He is something of a dandy, a social reformer, and he calls himself a writer, though his works never progress beyond the title page. He cannot work for a living because there is no job that will afford him both dignity and time for study. Rivas paints Emilio as an unmitigated idler and misfit, but he shows some sympathy for him in his conclusion:

> Yo me retiré pensando en ese infeliz joven inteligente y virtuoso que, ansioso de trabajar, se veía condenado a vivir, como un perdido, en las calles de Bogotá; y que la misma suerte corren infinidad de jóvenes que envían de los Estados a educarse en la Universidad, que conquistan ciencia y el título de doctores, y que no queriendo volver a sus pueblos, se quedan aquí, llevando una vida inútil y siendo un verdadero obstáculo para la sociedad.

In "Don Querubín el rico" (*El Neogranadino,* October 29, 1852) Rivas mercilessly sketches one of the satirist's inevitable subjects, the usurer, piling up grotesque detail to lay bare his whole miserable being. Don Querubín's greatest source of income is the government, to which he lends at twenty per cent. From his lesser clientele he extracts ten per cent monthly. His two diversions, since one is free and the other profitable, are worship and gambling, and he encourages his wife in her devoutness and his daughter in her dieting because fasting for either reason saves him money. His favorite maxims are "Tanto vales cuanto tienes" and "Cada uno para sí y Dios para todos." Rivas' physical description of the miser is a good example of the vitriolic style which makes the piece effective.

> Don Querubín es muy conocido por su cara de cuaresma, sus barbas descoloridas de miedo de que la cara les cobre usura, y

sus ojos, que han ido a habitar al cogote, por ser puesto más
barato, para poder alquilar las cuencas como almacenes; por su
sombrero de copa alta y levita, que algunos toman por grasa
cuando reparan el cuello, y otros por piel de rana, al verla tan
sin pelo.

A favorite subject of Spanish and Spanish American *costumbristas*, the miserable government employee, is sketched in "Don Zacarías el empleado" (*El Neogranadino*, December 3, 1852). Rivas shows him no more sympathy than is his usual lot.

Había en esta ciudad, en el año de 18 . . ., un joven que para
nada servía, que nada sabía y que nada quería aprender; y daba
por razón que el mucho estudio mata el ingenio, como el mucho
soplar apaga el fuego; pero necesitando recursos para sostenerse,
y siendo completamente inútil para el trabajo, no encontró otra
puerta abierta que la de los empleos, ancho y suntuoso templo
sostenido por la Patria para sus servidores, y que a veces llega a
ser hospital de inválidos para el mantenimiento de algunos inhábiles, perezosos e ignorantes.

Don Zacarías' only talent is for keeping himself in political favor at all times—at a presidential inauguration he congratulated the new president, then turned to the retiring president with "Yo saludo también al sol en Occidente." Rivas concludes:

Tal es la existencia de esa planta que llaman empleado, en
los tiempos caliginosos que atravesamos: planta azotada siempre
por contrarios vientos, y que, como las nacidas en los páramos,
tiene que estar siempre doblada para uno u otro lado.

In "Alfredo el estudiante" (*El Neogranadino*, December 24, 1852) Rivas criticizes education. Alfredo is the son of the "compadre del padrino del nieto de la suegra de mi hermana," sent from the provinces to the Colegio del Rosario in Bogotá. After several years of more extra-curricular than curricular activity, he graduated, not by properly concluding his course of law, but by a method he describes frankly.

En el estado de desorganización en que hoy se encuentran los
estudios, habiendo Universidades y colegios privados que dan
títulos, nadie debe estudiar ya, porque esto trae molestias, y lo
que se hace es presentarse en cualquier colegio, pagar la módica
propina y pedir que le armen a uno de Doctor. Yo me gradué al
fin, porque mis padres saboreen la dicha de verme de Doctor, y por
venir de Representante por mi Estado.

Rivas is not unsympathetic toward the boy, whom he describes as noble and generous; rather he criticizes the system which allows and encourages him to aspire to the title of "Doctor." He is also alarmed that a man no better equipped intellectually than Alfredo can and likely will become a provincial political leader.

The most sprightly of all Rivas' type sketches is that called "El comerciante," an ironic, first-person account of the life and passions of a merchant. The world is a stage, he says, and before finding himself in commerce he tried all the professions "para ver si en alguna me toca hacer de Rey, y en todas me he encontrado sólo de comparsa." Reduced to contemplation of suicide, the devil suggested to him that instead of himself he hang his fellow man, so he became a merchant, and he has found poetry, delight, excitement, and power. He caresses, arranges, and classifies his merchandise with the same pleasure as a priest his parishioners, a botanist his plants, a coquette her adornments, a general his battalions. His approach to a customer is like that of a lover:

> Un amante a los pies de su querida pidiéndole la felicidad, jurándole ferviente amor, constancia eterna y un porvenir de dicha y de ventura, hasta que consigue que ella, pálida, temblorosa y avergonzada, a pesar de su virtud y de sus creencias, consume su desgracia, es nada ante la elocuencia, la fascinación y el entusiasmo que empleo para dominar el corazón del comprador y obligarlo a que, a pesar de su miseria y de sus creencias, vacilante y atemorizado, consume su desgracia, comprando algo de lo que llamamos *muérganos*.

He peddles from house to house, raises prices for weddings and funerals, encourages profitable public holidays, optimistically seeks political influence. His one regret—a merchant has neither the time nor the heart for marriage; but he has sublimated this incongruous emotion by joining a club dedicated to the vilification of women. The sketch concludes with a parody of Espronceda's "Canción del pirata" which the merchant composed one day while counting his money. It begins:

> Con diez cajones por banda,
> Mucha ropa y caja fuerte,
> No espero, busco la suerte
> En mi querido almacén.

And the refrain:

> Que es mi tienda, mi tesoro,
> Es mi ley, el menudear,
> Mi Dios, la plata y el oro,
> Mi única dicha, engañar.

In "La beata" Rivas scourges the woman of ambition and pride who, unmarried and beyond hope of marriage, refuses to withdraw from society and elects religion as the pretext for her embittered machinations.

> La beata es el fiscal de todas las muchachas bonitas, y las persigue sin descanso. Es el demonio aterrador de los enamorados (por eso la detesto); la trompeta de la difamación de todas las de su sexo; el correo noticioso de todas las fiestas de iglesia; el telégrafo de comunicación de todas las desgracias domésticas; el pregonero de las desvergüenzas ocultas, y el más feroz enemigo de todo lo que es bello, noble y generoso.

All *beatas* have hydrophobia, says Rivas, and ought to be required to bathe and burn their clothing. The one thing they fear is water, and Rivas has devised an aqueous incantation (¡Agua por cara y pescuezo! ¡Agua por espalda y pecho! Quede el cochambre deshecho por siempre jamás. Amén.) to exorcise a *beata* who is presently persecuting him.

Rivas returns to a criticism of education in "Mi sobrina." A superficial formal education, lack of sensible instruction and control at home, and over-emphasis of social triviality have brought his sensitive young niece close to missing her chance for a happy and useful life.

> Adela tiene hermosos instintos, una alma apasionada y ama mucho a Alfredo; y entre esto y los vicios de su educación y las tontas exigencias de la sociedad, se ha establecido desde hoy una lucha a muerte.
>
> Veremos qué triunfa.

Rivas is much less sympathetic toward Adela's brother Recaredo in "Mi sobrino," but the satire is literary, not social. Recaredo was a stupid child who at school could learn only grammar, and it is not surprising, implies Rivas, that such a boy grew up to be an author and critic, one of those "a quienes Platón aconsejaba que se coronasen de flores y se desterrasen de la República por *inútiles y peor que inútiles*." Recaredo is a classicist, has a chlamys and a buskin on his desk and a portrait of Melpomene above it, and is furious with Racine for having written *Athalie* and *Esther*. Among his works are 675 sonnets to Venus, 40,000 pastoral songs, a trunk of Anacreontics, 3 epics, and 37 tragedies, but his real mania is for grammar.

> Pues han de saber ustedes que desde el siglo del gramático Zoilo para acá, no ha habido gramático como mi sobrino: es un metrogramático, que, a la manera del termómetro, marca maquinalmente y en el acto los grados gramaticales de todo lo que oye y todo lo que lee; o más bien, es un autómata gramatical, construído admirablemente para señalar los errores en la composición.

In short, he is unexcelled at finding fault. "Cuán triste me ha parecido el oficio de mi sobrino," comments Rivas, "buscando las manchas del sol de la inteligencia que derrama sobre nuestro suelo la luz, la virtud y la ciencia!"

Rivas' caricature of the petty, superficial, self-styled *literato* is rich in satire and humor and is one of his most suggestive articles. Curiously, Rivas inserts in the middle of his raillery what seems to be a serious romantic manifesto, but the ancient-modern quarrel is not his main concern, though his treatment of classicism suggests Mesonero's "El romanticismo y los románticos" in reverse.

Not all of Rivas' *costumbrista* articles have the form of the satirical type sketch. In fact, one, "El cosechero," uses the character sketch for a purely historical purpose. It records the *modus vivendi* of *taita* Ponce, a share-cropper in tobacco and a Rousseauesque natural man corrupted by work and money. The picture is realistic, with excellent examples of folk speech and psychology, and if it were not burdened with a romantic epilogue it would rival Restrepo's "Mi compadre Facundo" in artistry and interpretation.

Two purely descriptive *cuadros* demonstrate that description was not Rivas' forte. One, "Las fiestas de Piedras," in letter form, is a conventional treatment of the rural *fiesta*, emphasizing the grotesque, the quaint, and the sordid, too stiff and humorless to be recognized as Rivas' work. The other, "El San Pedro en Guataquisito," is similar and not much better, though it offers a novel theory about drunkenness as "el palacio de la verdad" and has a long and fascinating conversation by three drunken laborers.

In two articles Rivas pays his respects to the conventional personal essay. "A veranear" deals with a conventional subject, a family vacation in the "hot country," and the introduction mentions similar articles by José Manuel Groot ("Nos fuimos a Ubaque") and Ricardo Silva ("Mi familia viajando"). Rivas and his family seek "esa libertad tan ponderada del campo" in vain, for they find the same hypocrisy, trivial convention, and minute complication they had hoped to leave behind in the city. The article is written with good humor, as the form demanded, and it is given more than conventional depth by the satire of civilized mores in a rustic setting.

"Un paseo al campo," reminiscent of Caicedo Rojas' "Dos paseos al salto," follows the unoriginal formula of relating the embarrassing calamities suffered in the country by a city *cachaco*.

One of Rivas' most effective satirical articles, and his most ambitious and carefully planned, is "Contrariedades de un redactor," which, like "Mi sobrino," deals with the world of letters. A young man named Leoncio announces to Rivas his determination to found a new kind of periodical, one which will be "a la altura de la situación."

> Cuento con la eficaz cooperación de algunos amigos, y me propongo . . . abrir una nueva era para la prensa del país, evitando toda disputa estéril, toda polémica infecunda y toda rivalidad inútil.

Rivas tries to dissuade his young friend, assuring him that money, not talent, makes a newspaper, but Leoncio is resolute. The paper, *El Aegos Potamos,* announces itself as "Periódico científico, político y literario, de comercio, bellas artes y estadística," which, a study of Colombian papers will show, is not as ridiculously unreal a program as Rivas meant it to be. The paper's motto is "La prensa es un sacerdocio: los que lo ejercen merecen veneración."

Rivas makes good sport of the contents of the first number, in which each article is rhetorically dedicated to one of the editors. The "Statistics" department announces that the paper is counting the beggars in Bogotá, carries a table of deaths, and a listing of births—seven legitimate and 650 illegitimate. "Commerce" is covered by the announcement of the arrival of a shipment of goods which left Paris sixteen years before, the news that the telegraph is working as far as San Victorino, a suburb of Bogotá, and that merchants have invented raffles to sell at ten times its value merchandise that nobody wants. There is also a "Necrology" which ultimately proves the paper's undoing. It opens:

> La parca Atropos ha cortado inexorable el hilo de la vida del Sargento Prieto, cuando el tiempo, en su vuelo inmutable, marcaba ya casi veinte lustros, desde que la estrella del destino lo colocó en la mansión de los mortales.

The editors' vain delight with their first effort is clouded when, after three days, not a single subscription has been bought and even the most polite of those to whom the paper was sent have returned it. This, says Rivas, is an editor's first "contrariedad."

The second disillusionment comes with the arrival of exchanges and their reviews of *El Aegos Potamos*. In these Rivas cleverly satirizes the partisanship of the Bogotá press. Ironically, the reviews take notice only of the innocent "Necrology" which appeared on the back page. *El Fenix* takes the view of offended Christianity, alleging that the editors, like Julian the Apostate, are trying to revive paganism. *El Porvenir* represents romanticism: "Sobre los despojos de las edades . . . se ha levantado la religión del sentimiento y del dolor." *La Gaceta de los Dolientes,* the voice of science, holds that Sergeant Prieto could have been saved by hydropathic medicine. *La Luz* labels the necrology, and the press in general, infamous, subversive, immoral: "Qué será de los buenos, qué sera de la familia y de la tranquilidad doméstica!" Where *La Luz* sees radicalism and anarchy, *La Ley* detects military totalitarianism: "El pueblo no se deja engañar ya por oropeles y frases altisonantes, y destesta el despotismo militar." The masterpiece of all the reviews is that of *El Pastor Fido,* which limits its criticism to the egregious errors in semantics and classical lore; Rivas delightfully points up its pedantry by using Greek etyma, Latin quotations, and references to imposing scholarly titles in German and French.

The reaction of the editors of *El Aegos* is in character—with so many enemies to combat the paper must become a daily. But the printer demands payment for the first number (third disillusionment), and Leoncio tries unsuccessfully to hang himself—"última y no pequeña contrariedad de un redactor."

In this article Rivas reveals, with considerable exaggeration, to be sure, the unhappy state of journalism in Bogotá and points out factors contributing to the chaos: the editors' naiveté, spurious idealism, vanity, and triviality; and, above all, the unmitigated partisanship of everybody in the profession. The article was planned and written with greater care than is standard in *costumbrismo*; it stands out in this regard even among the articles of Rivas, and he was a better craftsman than most. The style is humorous, urbane, and free from bitterness.

Most of Rivas' articles, unlike those of Juan de Dios Restrepo, fall readily into three classifications—the type sketch, the satirical *artículo*, and the descriptive *cuadro*. He excels at the first and the second (especially "Contrariedades de un redactor"), but he hardly rises above conventionality in the descriptive genre.

Laverde Amaya says of Rivas:

> Nunca escribe tan sólo a impulsos del capricho . . . sino reducido por el encanto de la verdad, atraído irresistiblemente por la aspiración de ver corregidos los vicios sociales; delirando

siempre con el loable pensamiento de levantar el nivel moral o intelectual del hombre.[9]

This judgement stands up. Few of Rivas' articles lack a critical purpose, and most of them have far more than the average burden of ideas in subject, suggestion, and allusion. Whereas many of the *costumbristas* were merely amusing themselves genteelly, Rivas, as his care in form and style demonstrates, looked upon *costumbrismo* as an art worthy of concentration.

Compared with Restrepo, with whom he has a good deal in common as satirist and social critic, Rivas is less cynical, less intense, and probes less deeply into the social organism, but he has a greater variety of satirical techniques—vitriolic scorn, measured irony, sympathetic ridicule, and good-humored raillery —and he has the essential lightness of touch which Restrepo never achieves. Even when most severe he holds fast to his sense of humor.

Rivas shows a considerable degree of sophistication for his time. He is happily free from the superficial "sweetness and light," the saccharine nostalgia, the withdrawn cult of the quaint which are endemic to the *costumbrista*. He always writes as a man of reason, critical of abuse and sham, unprejudiced, and sincere, and in his realistic optimism he is a good deal more urbane than Restrepo.

In short, for the consistent quality of his articles, for his happy choice of subjects, for his ability as writer and satirist, and for the rationality of his criteria, Rivas ranks as one of the best of Colombian *costumbristas*.

THE PRE-MOSAICOS

The writers discussed above are the most important of those who were active before the appearance of *El Mosaico* in 1858. Consideration of their work leaves little doubt that Colombian *costumbrismo* is a direct product of the movement in Spain, and shows, further, that the sketch of manners was born almost full-grown in Colombia and experienced little evolution in basic form in the twenty years before 1860.

For example, the use of the familiar essay as a humorous-satirical form, first found in the early anonymous "Fiestas," is continued, and somewhat refined, in such articles as "Nos fuimos a Ubaque" (Groot), "Dos paseos al salto" (Caicedo), and "Mo-

---

[9] *Fisonomías*, p. 221.

tivo por el cual" (Ortiz). The same form is put to a more critical use by Caicedo in "El Duende en un baile" and by Restrepo in "Una botella de brandi i otra de jinebra." The satirical treatment of character types, which began with Gutiérrez Vergara's "Cachaco," is carried forward and greatly improved by Restrepo's "Los pepitos" and, most notably, by Rivas' long series of type portraits. Of the satirical *artículo*, which also originated in Colombia with Gutiérrez Vergara, there are many examples in the pre-Mosaico period—"Las contrariedades de un redactor" (Rivas) is certainly the best. There are many good specimens of the descriptive *cuadro*, of which Gutiérrez Vergara's "El aguinaldo" is an early example. "La tienda de Don Antuco" (Groot), "Una taza de chocolate" (Ortiz), and "Mi compadre Facundo" (Restrepo) are outstanding among them.

A very large proportion of the articles mentioned in this chapter are satirical-critical, or properly *artículos de costumbres* as defined by Tarr, and the *cuadros*, or primarily descriptive and expository pieces, are in the minority. This leads to the conclusion that the sketch in the early years was looked upon as an essentially critical genre. This is doubtless due to the influence of Larra and the early articles of Mesonero. It will be seen that in the later period the trend was to the descriptive *cuadro* and satire was generally neglected.

The production of the pre-Mosaico period is very uneven in quality, as might be expected. The authors who stand out for their general high quality are Restrepo and Rivas. Santander contributes the least. The others—Caicedo, Groot, Ortiz—have at least one or two really good articles. However, the quality and quantity of sketches of this period are sufficient to demonstrate that Colombian writers had mastered the genre before the advent of the Mosaicos, whose name is almost synonymous with *costumbrismo* among Colombians.

III
THE MOSAICO CIRCLE

Discussion of the *costumbrista* movement in Colombia in the years of its greatest flourishing, 1860 to 1870, requires frequent reference to a group of writers who were known as Mosaicos, or the Mosaico. The Mosaico is the most famous of all Colombian literary *tertulias*, and, though it was not a literary school in any sense, espoused no theories, and had no fixed membership, organization, or meeting place, it was a sort of alma mater to most of the young *literatos* of the era. Its influence on letters was great.

The Mosaico was born, though nobody at once realized it, when Rafael Eliseo Santander early in 1858 invited a group of younger men to his home "a tomar chocolate de media canela, fumar, y mentir, de cuatro a seis horas, como decía el canónigo Saavedra." Later the group met frequently at the home of José María Samper, but a meeting was likely to occur any night of the week at the home of any of the *contertulianos*. The circle was known as the Mosaico, and the meetings as *mosaicos* after the appearance of the periodical called *El Mosaico*, the informal organ of the group.

The nucleus of the Mosaico was José María Vergara y Vergara, Samper, José Manuel Marroquín, José María Quijano Otero, and Manuel Pombo, all writers prominently mentioned in histories of Colombian literature. Others of the group, less regular but no less distinguished, were Miguel Samper, Salvador Camacho Roldán, Ricardo Silva, Diego Fallon, Jorge Isaacs, José David Guarín, José Joaquín Borda, Juan de Dios Restrepo, and Juan Francisco Ortiz. Almost all of them were from thirty to thirty-five years old in 1858.

The only aspects typical of the meetings were the rich chocolate that was invariably served and a complete informality. The program was allowed to develop as spirits were moved, a little like a Quaker meeting, perhaps, but certainly with more ebullience. Since all members were writers, much time was given to reading and criticizing new compositions, but there was apparently never any danger that the group might come to take itself too seriously. José Manuel Marroquín said, years later:

> Dímonos a esos entretenimientos literarios sin fe ninguna en nuestra propia literatura, y habiéndonos con los versos y las letras como años antes nos habíamos habido con las cometas y los trompos, esto es, como meros instrumentos de diversión. . . . Entre nosotros jamás se habló del genio, ni del arte, ni de psicología, ni de soñadores, ni de estética, ni de lo ideal, ni de lo transcendente, ni de lo subjetivo, ni de tantas cosas así.[1]

Only one topic of conversation was forbidden—politics. At a time when revolutions were an almost annual occurrence politics was not a suitable subject for urbane conversation. Men of both principal parties participated in the Mosaico.

The Mosaico is reputed to have operated as a sympathetic tribunal to which novice authors might bring their work for appraisal, and members insisted that they did all within their power to encourage and improve Colombian letters. Their proudest achievement in this regard was the discovery of the novelist Jorge Isaacs, though they discovered him as a poet. Without the encouragement of the Mosaicos, Marroquín tells us, Isaacs would never have written *María*, the romantic novel that still enjoys continental fame.

To understand the importance of the Mosaico circle for the development of *costumbrismo*, it is necessary only to examine the list of members. Of those mentioned most frequently as regular participants in the sessions, at least half are *costumbristas* of some renown. That the meetings often took the form of a round table on *costumbrismo* there can be little doubt, and it is reasonable to assume that the quantity and quality of essays of manners were favorably affected. The frequency with which the members of the Mosaico dedicated their articles to one another, or wrote an article of rebuttal or supplement to that of another member, implies a lively interest and even a rivalry in the writing of *costumbrismo*. Such competition must have had primarily beneficial effects, though it may also have contributed to the spirit of improvisation that dominated the movement, often to its detriment.

But the Mosaico's greatest contribution to the *costumbrista* movement was the magazine from which the group got its name. Its founders and most of its contributors were *costumbristas*, it owed its origin to an interest in *costumbrismo*, and a large

---

[1] Quoted by Marroquín's son in *Don José Manuel Marroquín íntimo* (Bogotá: Arboleda y Valencia, 1915), p. 170.

proportion of the more significant sketches treated in this study were first published in it.

The periodical *El Mosaico* was founded only a few months after the organization of the *tertulia*. The editors give credit for its conception to Eugenio Díaz, an unlettered, rustic novelist who one day appeared in Vergara's study in a poncho and panama hat, with a manuscript novel under his arm, to propose the establishment of a literary periodical which would publish some of Díaz' sketches of manners. Vergara read part of the manuscript and was convinced. The first number of the paper appeared three days later—December 24, 1858.

Díaz, however, was never one of the editors of *El Mosaico*—it might be alleged that Díaz, a rustic only slightly more schooled than the subjects of his *cuadros*, was too little sophisticated to be editor of an urbane magazine. In any case, the charter editors were Vergara, Ricardo Carrasquilla, Marroquín, and José Joaquín Borda. They were joined a few weeks later by José David Guarín and Ezequiel Uricoechea, the latter of whom was in charge of the scientific section which appeared in the paper irregularly.

El Mosaico was a weekly, appearing at first on Saturday and later on Wednesday, consisting of eight pages *in octavo*, two columns to the page. The first volume ran to December 24, 1859, and Volume II from January 7, 1860, to December 29, 1860. Publication was interrupted at this point by civil war, to be resumed three years later. Volume III ran from January 13, 1864, to January 14, 1865. After thirty-six numbers in Volume IV the paper succumbed again with the issue of November 16, 1865. A third and less important revival of the paper ran for a year beginning in January, 1871.

In time the paper came to have a really national character. The editors boasted that there was not a single writer in Bogotá who had not contributed to it, and many outside the capital were also contributors. A list published in the first number of Volume III includes many writers in the provinces, one in Ecuador, and three in the United States.

A number of factors make *El Mosaico* remarkable. No other literary publication of its time in Colombia can approach it in length of life, in distinction and variety of contributors, or in relative excellence of content and form, and it is virtually certain that no other unsubsidized paper of the century can boast of not having lost money. It is particularly valuable as a mirror of the tastes, the criteria, the naive curiosity, the general level of culture, and the manners of mid-century Colombia. The literature of Colombia of the last half of the nineteenth century would surely have been a good deal poorer without the stimulus provided by this modestly charming little magazine.[2]

---

[2] A complete file of *El Mosaico* is a scarce item. One was destroyed with the Ministerio de Relaciones Exteriores during the revolt of the spring of 1948. Another complete set is in the Instituto Caro y Cuervo in Bogotá. Harvard has the first two numbers of Volume I, and Duke has Volumes II and III entire and in good condition. The University of North Carolina has the complete run on microfilm.

IV
THE MOSAICO WRITERS

Among the *costumbrista* writers associated with *El Mosaico*, Vergara, Marroquín, Guarín (who were editors of the paper), and Ricardo Silva were the most significantly productive. Others who contributed to the genre through the columns of *El Mosaico* were Eugenio Díaz, José Joaquín Borda, Manuel Pombo, Ricardo Carrasquilla, and José María Samper. Many of these authors continued to write of manners long after the demise of *El Mosaico*, but their work has been regarded as a product of the Mosaico circle regardless of where or when it was published.

VERGARA

José María Vergara y Vergara (1831-1872) was a native *bogotano*, educated principally in the Jesuit seminary of the capital, and served as teacher, university administrator, and legislator in Popayán and Bogotá. In 1869, despondent at his wife's death, he went to France, where he made a sentimental pilgrimage to Chateaubriand's tomb, and to Spain, where he induced the Spanish Academy to authorize him to establish a corresponding body in Colombia. The Academia Colombiana de la Lengua, the first of the American academies, was founded under Vergara's direction in 1871. Vergara died less than a year later.

Including *El Mosaico*, Vergara founded, edited, or contributed to a dozen papers and periodicals, but not all his literary accomplishment was journalistic. His *Historia de la literatura en Nueva Granada* (Bogotá, 1867) is still the standard reference for the colonial period; the second part, dealing with the independence era, was lost in manuscript after his death. He wrote four novels, one of which—*Olivos y aceitunos, todos son unos* (1868)—is an important novel of manners, verse, essays, travel accounts, and biographical sketches, and he edited the *Museo de cuadros de costumbres*, one of the best *costumbrista* anthologies. Vergara's numerous articles on manners have been collected many times, usually with his literary and miscellaneous essays.[1]

---

[1] The best edition is *Obras escogidas* (Bogotá: Editorial Minerva, 1931); Volume XXIV of the Selección Samper Ortega is titled *Las tres tazas y otros cuadros*.

One of Vergara's few humorous personal essays, which is only vaguely *costumbrista*, is "El último Abencerraje, o biografías de mis caballos," recounting the author's many efforts to acquire and keep a good horse. It is reasonably successful as humor—though the pun is overworked—but occasional asides on politics and economics constitute its only manners interest. It first appeared in *El Mosaico*, September 3, 1864.

The equine motif appears again in "Consejos a mi potro," in which Vergara comments on the vices of his countrymen, and mankind in general, in the guise of advice to a colt about to be broken for the saddle. It is a whimsical piece, the studied naiveté of which is an effective background for Vergara's sharp observations on politics and society.

"Los buitres" (*El Mosaico*, December 24, 1864) is difficult to classify. It has elements of satire, personal reminiscence, and manners. The article is based on the author's childhood fascination with a family of vultures that nested on a hill near his country home. He professes that his observation of them gave him a valuable lesson in understanding and tolerance:

> Muchos años después, al presenciar de cerca los frenéticos odios de la política ... me he dicho: "ese hombre que pintan tan odioso y carnicero, tan depravado y tan sin corazón, ¿cómo será entre su casa? ... Yo he visto a los buitres en la vida privada cerrar sus uñas para acariciar a sus hijos: así son y serán también los hombres. Para destruír un odio, vencer una enemistad, no hay como ir valientemente a buscar al enemigo en el seno del hogar doméstico. A la luz de la llama del hogar que congrega en su derredor la familia, no se puede aborrecer a nadie...."

The logic is a little romantic, but perhaps the moral is valid.

The political satire of this article, though more implicit than overt, is bitter to the point of grotesqueness, but in spite of that the general tone is bucolically idyllic. Vergara longs for the manorial atmosphere of the family *hacienda* of his happy boyhood and praises the easy master-servant relationship which the advent of "democracy" has destroyed, repeatedly displaying the standard "good-old-days" romanticism. Also romantic is the pervading air of languid disillusionment; the prospect of death, Vergara says, "ahora no me repugna: aunque me convierta en lacre, lo mismo da." He even quotes Espronceda's "Que haya un cadáver más, ¿qué importa al mundo?" However, "Los buitres," though not strictly a *cuadro de costumbres*, is one of Vergara's best articles. It was obviously planned and composed with great affection and it is written in careful, precise, intimate language. It reveals a great deal about the author.

"Esquina de avisos," which also first appeared in *El Mosaico*, is a satirical article of a very different kind. In it Vergara criticizes *bogotanos* for their mania for publishing.

> La *anunciatividad* es el órgano mas prominente en la calavera del siglo XIX. Todo se publica. Un cliente escribe: *Una sentencia contra lei escrita*, i me pone a los jueces como nuevecitos. Un perdulario larga un folletito bajo este título: *Juzguen los hombres de honor*. Un Perico el de los Palotes, a propósito de un altercado con el Pedro Fernández de su suegro, este otro: *Al universo civilizado*.

The offense, as a look at a few periodicals of the time will reveal, is not exaggerated and the criticism is justified. Vergara is amused also at the tendency to post public announcements always on the same street corners—" a semejanza de los potros que no ejecutan ciertas operaciones sino donde mismo las ejecutó el anterior . . . así el hombre pone sus inmundicias morales unas sobre otras." The superimposed announcements on these walls create an effect like this:

> LA MUJER DE DOS MARIDOS—Ha muerto la señora Ulpiana Rodríguez! su aflijido esposo, sus inconsolables deudos, suplican a sus amigos que concurran a—EL ELIXIR DE AMOR, i luego se cantará por la señorita Mazzetti la graciosa tonadilla: *quién quiere mi naranjanita?*—SE NECESITA—EL HOMBRE DE—HIERRO— . . . Proclama del presidente a sus habitantes—DETRAS DE LA CRUZ EL DIABLO—Se ha perdido un niño de edad de—LA COMPAÑIA LIRICA—Se ha encontrado un anillo de oro con rubíes: la persona que lo hubiere perdido ocurra a—UN BANDOLERO DE MAJISTRADO. . . .

Vergara concludes: "Qué dice usted ahora, señor lector? No son *las esquinas de avisos* una copia fiel del estado en que están todas las cabezas?" The humor here is excellent and the style racy and colloquial, and the result is a sprightly article. It is less personal and moral than is the *costumbrista*'s wont and is the better for it.

The bulk of Vergara's production in manners is primarily descriptive, though often with elements of satire. One of the earliest, which appeared in the first volume of *El Mosaico*, is "El mercado de la Mesa," a description in three parts of the weekly market in a town fifty miles west of Bogotá. The first part follows the mule train of Manuel Fetecua, laden with beef, potatoes, and flour, from the *sabana* of Bogotá down to La Mesa. The second section treats in the same manner the caravan of Cupertino Farfán, who comes up from the more tropical south with cacao and rice, and the third deals with the market itself. Vergara's local color is wealthy in detail. The preparation of the beef, the loading of the mules, the line of march, overnight stops, the dress of the Indians encountered along the route, the nature and value of the merchandise in the market, and the character and activities of La Mesa's most colorful citizens—all of this is described with minute exactness.

The article suffers from impertinent interpolations and abrupt transitions, and the style is humorless and undistinguished, but the piece has value for the scope of its subject and its detailed observation; it is a documentary treatment of an important segment of provincial life.

In an article written several years later Vergara treats another provincial festival—"La semana santa en Popayán." It was apparently written for the anthology of *costumbrismo*, *Museo de cuadros de costumbres*, edited by Vergara in 1866. The emphasis here is on evocation of spirit rather than on physical detail. In the introduction Vergara reviews the history and geography of the city. His comment on the climate is charming:

> Su clima . . . sabeis cuál es su clima? El sabio Cáldas tomó la tarea de fijar las alturas, latitudes i climas de todos los lugares del Virreinato . . . i al llegar a Popayán . . . apuntó, en vez de un número una frase. "Parece, dijo, un clima inventado por los poetas."

In describing the processions which occur every night during Holy Week, Vergara makes little effort to distinguish one from the other, for he is less interested in photographic detail than in commemorating the devoutness of the city.

> Todos rezan en silencio, porque en ninguna parte hai mas devocion que en Popayan; i así es que las procesiones, que son todas nocturnas, en lugar de ser fuentes de abusos protejidos por las sombras de la noche, como sucederia en Bogotá, son por el contrario, una diversion perfectamente decorosa para los que tienen la desgracia de ser indiferentes o incrédulos, i una edificacion saludable para los que tenemos la dicha de creer.

The whole article, which is written with grace and conviction, is a hymn of faith, a lyric tribute to the traditional devotion of Popayán, and it is successful in spite of interpolations which tend to break the spell.

In "El lenguaje de las casas" (*El Mosaico*, January 7 and April 29, 1865) Vergara describes three houses belonging to three periods—the "casa santafereña," or colonial house; that of the early independence when the capital was known as Santafé de Bogotá; and "la casita nueva," scorned for its diminutiveness and fragility, belonging to the Bogotá or contemporary period. These houses are described in minute detail, and the choice of detail unmistakably characterizes the tastes, manners, and spirit of the eras to which the houses belong.

Though there is no narrative or dialogue, the article has life, a life created by lightness of tone and imaginative figures and phraseology. Vergara says of the papaya trees in a patio of the colonial house:

> En los corrales se ven papayos de troncos gordiflones abonados con cascajo, que con las manos en la cintura, la frente alta y la cabellera en desorden, parecen campesinos que se quedan viendo una torre en la ciudad.

The French lithographs which dominate the *décor* of the second house are "estampas de esas que han creado los franceses con el objeto de probar que las minas de bermellón y verdacho son inagotables."

The third part of the article is satirical, for the "casita nueva" is to Vergara the symbol of the contemporary break with hallowed tradition. The tiny house, built from materials left over from the construction of a real house, is so small that a candle extinguished in the bedroom can be smelled from one end of the house to the other. Vergara is equally scornful of the insubstantiality of the furnishings and the exotic tastes of the inhabitants. "La casa es un curioso museo de todos los objetos que se pueden romper. Pudiera escribirse *Fragility, thy name is extranjero*." But the flowers in the house have his sarcastic approval—"Las flores son hermosas hasta cuando son de moda."

Vergara omits mention of the inhabitants of his three houses except at the end of each section. At the end of the first part, for example, he asks the reader:

> ¿Tiene curiosidad de conocer a las personas que la habitan? Pues por la descripción de la casa puede asignarles fisonomía, edad, costumbres, vestidos, etc. Y viva seguro de que no se equivocará ni en un cinco por ciento.

Ricardo Silva accepted Vergara's challenge and, in an article called "Tres visitas," successfully described the occupants.

"El lenguaje de las casas" is a credit to Vergara. Stylistically it is one of his best pieces, almost without fault. Interest never flags throughout its more than twenty pages of unrelieved description. Above all, the article graphically epitomizes the tastes of three generations of *bogotanos*.

The best known of all Vergara's *costumbrista* essays, "Las tres tazas," uses a similar device. In it the polite manners of the same three periods are tied to the fashionable drink of each era. The "Taza primera" is an account of a soiree in the elegant home of the Marqués de San Jorge in 1813, at which most of the guests are heroes of the currently successful struggle for independence, the principal entertainment is the *contradanza*, and the featured refreshment is Spanish chocolate.

> ¡Musa de Grecia, la de las ingeniosas ficciones, hazme el favor de decirme cómo diablos se pudiera hacer llegar a las narices de mis actuales conciudadanos el perfume de aquel chocolate colonial!
> ... Pero el sabor de aquel chocolate era igual a su perfume; la cucharilla de plata entraba en el blando seno de la jícara con dificultad. No se hacían *buches* de chocolate como ahora, nó; ni se tomaba de prisa, ni con los ojos abiertos y el espíritu cerrado.

Vergara's "Taza segunda" is a cup of coffee, and he blames the British for it—"Con Bolívar vinieron los ingleses de la legión británica, y con ellos, cosa triste! el uso del café." It is served at the home of Juan de las Viñas in 1848, in a dining room where there is little elegance:

> La mesa en que comía todos los días el señor de las Viñas, rodeado de sus hijos como una viña de sus vástagos, era a propósito para aquella parra y aquellas viñas, pero insuficiente para los convidados, y se había tomado el partido de agregarle varias mesitas. Las que eran muy bajas se habían alzado sobre ladrillos, y aunque tambaleaban como Edda delante de su amado, éste no era mucho inconveniente; pero las que habían quedado altas tenían la ventaja de la solidez en cambio de la abominable joroba que imprimían al mantel.

The conduct of the guests, including the author, is no less grotesque, for, finding distasteful the acrid coffee so proudly served by Viñas, they demand and are served chocolate, whereupon "la escena se convirtió rápidamente en una escena de confianza." The shouting, singing, and dancing continue until four in the morning.

In the "Taza tercera" Vergara returns to the theme of the third part of "El lenguaje de las casas"—the contemporary vogue for everything foreign and the abhorrence of all that is Colombian. The host, the Marquis de Gacharná, described as a "francesito" from Boyacá, received his title and Norwegian citizenship in return for serving as Norwegian consul. "El gozo de monsieur de Gacharná al saber que ya no era colombiano fue limitado como su entendimiento, pero profundo como su gravedad." The marquis and his wife strive to create a foreign atmosphere about them, are uncivil to ordinary Colombians, and live penuriously to save for their occasional "elegant" receptions, to which Colombians are rarely invited. Vergara is forced by the marquis to drink three cups of tea, which he considers only a sudorific, and finds the dancing repulsive—"se bailó un muy indecente baile cuyo nombre ignoro y que consiste en bailar extremadamente abrazados, con otras circunstancias deplorables." Conversation was restricted to the war in Austria, the policies of Napoleon, and Paris fashions and "a cada cuatro palabras en mal español, se decían tres en mal francés."

Vergara summarizes:

En 1813 se convidaba a tomar una *taza de chocolate*, en taza de plata, y había baile, alegría, elegancia y decoro.

En 1848 se convidaba a tomar una *taza de café*, en taza de loza, y había *bochinche*, juventud, cordialidad y decoro.

En 1866 se convida a tomar una *taza de te en familia*, y hay silencio, equívocos indecentes, bailes de parva, ninguna alegría y mucho tono.

Espero que ... en 1880 se me convidará a *tomar quinina entre amigos*. Están de moda los sudoríficos y antiespasmódicos; ¿por qué no les ha de llegar su sanmartín a los febrífugos y antihepáticos?

How merciful that Vergara missed the age of the Coca Cola!

"Las tres tazas" seems to deserve the attention it has received. Few articles cover so much ground and give so much information so pleasantly. The clothing, entertainment, refreshments, and conversations of three eras are described in detail and the tone of polite society in each period is adequately characterized, in spite of some exaggeration for humorous effect and the author's aristocratic impatience with "progress." The humor is sometimes a little labored—there is at least one inexcusable pun—but it is generally sprightly enough to sustain interest in an uncommonly long article.

Vergara has two character sketches of quality. The first of them, "El correísta," which appeared in the first and third numbers of *El Mosaico*, eulogizes Don Marcos, the bearer of the mails between Bogotá and a provincial capital two hundred miles to the south. This courier is not the romantic horseman of our "pony express," but a marathon hiker who drives a humble mule before him. Vergara presents him as an indispensable public servant, esteemed, proud, and courageous, haste and efficiency personified.

> Atroz es la vida del correísta durante el largo camino al través de climas ardientes; sus horas están contadas, y el más ligero descanso entre día viniera a formarle un retardo de dos horas al fin de su destino, hora que se tomaría severamente en cuenta y le acarrearía una rebaja en su exiguo sueldo. Almuerza y come de pie y dando vueltas en derredor de su mula cargada que nunca abandona. . . . Desde que llega al principio de la bajada que va a terminar en la casa donde acostumbra desayunarse o comer, comienza a llamar gritando a la casera, antigua conocida:
> —¡Eh, señora Chepa! ¡que me asen un pedazo de carne . . .! ¡apure, que el administrador es el que come sentado y duerme la siesta! ¡El cacao, no se olvide, señora Chepa, que voy de prisa!
> Y dando estas voces va bajando, y cuando llega, la señora Chepa que estaba con el oído alerta y oyó sus voces a tiempo, ya le tiene sobre el mostrador lo que ha pedido.

This air of haste is effectively developed into a kind of beat, an ever-quickening tempo which shapes and characterizes the actions and personality of Don Marcos. Though the article shows some evidence of hasty composition—the conclusion is tritely contrived—the style is well suited to the subject, moving swiftly and smoothly with the urgency of the action. Realistic colloquial dialogue contributes to the pace of the article and sharply etches the figure of Don Marcos. Vergara here achieves a fascinating characterization of a colorful individual at the same time that he records an exotic feature of regional manners, hence "El correísta" is one of those too rare efforts in which subject and execution join hands to create a brightly informative and interesting *cuadro*.

A sketch of equal charm, and one of Vergara's best known, is "El chino de Bogotá," which describes with indulgent affection the ubiquitous urchin of the Bogotá street, a subject much less heroic but no less engaging than the *correísta*. Alberto, Vergara's *chino*, left his unmarried mother at the age of four and attached himself to a shoemaker, with whom he stayed, in spite of mistreatment, until he was seven, the age of majority for a *chino*.

> Nada más simpático ni más feo que la figura de Alberto el día en que se declaró mayor de edad y sin generales con la sociedad. Poco crecido, pues los chinos de mayor estatura jamás pasan de vara y media, con unos dientes tan anchos que casi llenaban todo el frente de su boca grande y respondona; con las orejas grandes por los castigos aplicados a esta parte de su cuerpo que él no estimaba en nada; con un par de ojos chiquitos pero inteligentes y

chispeantes; unos pies en que se habían refugiado todas las niguas de Bogotá; patizambo y *rodillijunto*, a causa del mal grado con que lo llevó su madre en su seno . . . tal era y es el retrato de aquel héroe de incógnitas aventuras.

Later Vergara completes the description by indicating that the boy's soul is no more prepossessing than the flesh:

Solamente la fe, esa gran virtud, ese sublime y santo despotismo de las almas, puede hacer creer que el *chino* está salvado y redimido con la sangre del Redentor del mundo. No parece *chino* sino el pecado mortal en persona, el pecado *patojo* y maligno.

The body of the article consists of incidents and adventures which reveal the *chino*'s method of subsistence, his cunning at petty thievery and bald deception of all kinds, his impudence, scorn of dignity, incorrigible perversity, and, above all, his sublime independence; a riot in congress incited by Alberto's well-timed, derisive whistle during a speech is related in delightful detail. The active career of the *chino* ends at age eighteen, Vergara says, but he retains until death something of the *chino* spirit—"su última palabra es un chiste, y se despide de la vida y del padre confesor tan desenfadadamente como ha vivido." Vergara's article is one of the best on the subject—Ricardo Silva's "El niño Agapito" is a rival—and a valuable contribution to a gallery of Bogotá types and a biography of the *pícaro* in the new world.

Although there is considerable variation in quality and manner, Vergara's articles are all good for one reason or another. At times he writes deliberately and carefully, and the result is the stately grace of "Los buitres" or the suggestion of "El lenguaje de las casas"; sometimes a more spontaneous approach produces the sprightly simplicity of "El correísta" or the gay triviality of "Esquina de avisos." But there are lapses even in his most polished pieces and at worst his style can be as tedious as in "El mercado de la Mesa." There is generally restraint in his informality and his language is rarely colloquial. His humor is usually adequate to his purpose though sometimes forced and contrived. He uses effectively a fine sense of irony, and a few of his articles—"Esquina de avisos" for example—are whimsically witty. He seldom undertakes sustained satire, and when he does it is heavily diluted, as in "Consejos a mi potro," but there is effective satire in some of his descriptive articles and he is adept at incidental satire in the form of epigrammatic observation.

Vergara's gift is for observation and description, and it would be difficult to find more lively description than that of "El lenguaje de las casas," but he is not infallible, for his hand is heavy in the documentary detail of "El mercado de la Mesa." Probably no other *costumbrista* of Colombia is as impressive for his contribution to the documentation of nineteenth-century manners, for most of his articles are invaluable simply for their content.

Vergara is not the planner that Silva is, a stylist like Marroquín, a satirist like Restrepo, nor an outstanding humorist, but he combines these qualities to a degree sufficient to afford him distinction.

MARROQUÍN

José Manuel Marroquín (1827-1908) was the most long-lived of the Colombian *costumbristas* and one of the most prolific. He was a charter member of the Mosaico group and one of the editors of *El Mosaico*. He was orphaned as an infant and reared by his grandmother and several aunts and uncles on the family ranch, Yerbabuena, near Bogotá. He was relatively wealthy and most of his life was devoted to scholarship, writing, and teaching. He was acting president of the Republic from 1898 to 1904 and has often been unjustly blamed for Colombia's loss of Panama. He was a founding member of the Academia Colombiana, and, in addition to *El Mosaico*, wrote for *La Biblioteca de Señoritas, La Caridad, El Zipa, El Repertorio Colombiano*, and *El Papel Periódico Ilustrado*.

In addition to many *artículos de costumbres*, Marroquín is the author of four novels, one of which, *El Moro* (1897), the autobiography of a horse, still is read, and his *Tratado de ortografía castellana* (1858) is reputed to have been effective in counteracting the chaotic "reforms" in spelling.

Almost all of Marroquín's *costumbrista* articles, which are available in several collections, contain a satirical or critical element, but some, especially the earlier pieces, are predominantly descriptive or humorous. Such an article is "Vamos a misa al pueblo" (*El Mosaico*, September 5, 1860), in which the author stands with the reader on the balcony of the rectory and gives a colorful account of the peripheral activities of Sunday mass in a small town, emphasizing the social and commercial importance of this weekly assembly of all the people in the district. The reader sees Don Narciso reading the news on the town hall steps;

Don Pascual leading a political argument; the tavern overflowing with customers; horse-trading; a group lingering outside the church to time their entrance with the end of the sermon; another group—"los más ilustrados"—abstaining from mass altogether. It is a vivid picture of motion and color, a panorama depicting the mind and soul of a whole community. There are nice satirical touches: Don Narciso, nicknamed "El Código" for his knowledge of the law, "es hombre que tiene a su *señora indispuesta* en vez de *tener mala a su mujer*"; the *tinterillo*, or petty-grafting lawyer, the ladies in too expensive dresses, and the dandy whose elegance belies his bankruptcy.

In "Al señor Ricardo Carrasquilla" (*El Mosaico*, September 5, 1850), a commentary and supplement to Carrasquilla's "Lo que va de ayer a hoy," Marroquín adds details to Carrasquilla's comparison of present and past schools. The substance of the article is reminiscence, but part of its purpose is to criticize contemporary schools and their precocious pupils. The latter, he says, have too much freedom and privilege, become sophisticated before their time, and "han de ser un poco empalagosos a los diez y ocho años, y de todo punto insoportables a los veinticinco." With excellent irony he comments on "modern" methods of education:

. . . Pues es fuerte cosa que a un niño que prefiere hacer sus cuentas con rayas hechas en la pared, se le obligue por medio de la fuerza brutal a aprender la adicion, la sustraccion y la regla de tres, y a valerse de todos los medios que, segun la opinion privada de los matemáticos, son propios para descubrir las relaciones de los números.

The form of the article is not good, since it is a sort of memorandum to Carrasquilla, but the picture of school life is rewarding and the criticism, though ultra-conservative, rings true.

"Recuerdos del campo" is also based on reminiscence. It opens with the lyric affirmation that life in the country is "un cielo anticipado, una *sucursal* del Paraíso," and then laments that thanks to the spreading commercialism of *yankismo* the old love of the land and the wholesome customs it engendered are rapidly disappearing. The body of the article enumerates the lost delights of the author's boyhood in the country, dwelling at length on the annual roundup and branding. Even the odor of seared flesh under the branding iron is dear to Marroquín—"A mi me deleita el que se me quemen los bigotes al encender un cigarro, porque cuantas veces me sucede, me huele a rodeos."

The conclusion of the *cuadro* is a description of Yerbabuena, Marroquín's beloved home. It is a labor of love.

"El cuarto de los trastos" is also an exercise in reminiscence, though it begins with a condemnation of the "casita moderna," a house too small to have a room to receive *trastos*, the useless effects of house and family that are too good to be destroyed. Such a room was one of the glories of the old "casa santafereña," and in it a curious child, like the frequent reader of the *Quijote*, could always find something new, something previously unnoticed. Most of the article, which is suggestive and modestly humorous, is a whimsical inventory of objects cast into the room by past generations, many of which recall a forgotten custom or incident.

A few of Marroquín's articles may be classified as humorous personal essays. One of these, "La carrera de mi sobrino" (*El Mosaico*, April 16, 1864), recounts the frustrations of the author's hapless nephew—and *costumbrista* nephews are always hapless—in his efforts to find a vocation. It seems to have been written only for fun, and the humorous potential of the impact of unyielding reality on an unqualified youth is skillfully exploited.

Another casual divertisement is "El domingo por la mañana," which details the author's frustrated attempt to write an article at home on Sunday morning. It has the form of a letter to his editor explaining his failure. The humor is stereotyped, the subject is commonplace, and the motif—the excuse for not writing the article is the article itself—is tiresomely frequent in *costumbrismo*.

Most of Marroquín's articles have satire as their basic purpose, and the satirical articles conveniently fall into an early group, written before the author was forty, in which the touch is light and humor prevails, and a later series marked by real didactic zeal.

"Contribuciones directas" (*La Biblioteca de Señoritas*, 1859) is a kind of complaint about the obligation society forces on the rich man and which the rich man accepts out of vanity. Marroquín claims to have contributed money, in a single day, to a home for *señoras vergonzantes*, a bridge he will never use, a benefit for an actress he has never seen, a *fiesta* for a saint he has never heard of, a destitute schoolmate, etc. But he does not feel bitter, only used.

"Penitencia" (*El Mosaico*, 1859) is a pleasing satire on domestic manners inspired in the phrase, "Quédese U. a hacer la penitencia," the standard form for inviting a caller to stay on for dinner. "Take potluck with us." Marroquín sees clearly the problem posed by such an invitation:

> La parte *convidante*, en tanto que pronuncia la fórmula o aguarda la respuesta, ruega interiormente a todos los santos de su devocion, si es que tiene devocion a algunos santos, no permitan que la invitacion se acepte. La parte convidada casi nunca ignora esto, y, ademas, echa de ver que el comer fuera de su casa trastorna más o ménos los planes que habia formado para el dia y el órden de sus ocupaciones; así es que nunca deja de esforzarse por encontrar buenas excusas.

But custom demands that the invitation be offered insistently and urbanity prohibits obstinate refusal; the result is inconvenience, embarrassment, and indigestion for all concerned. The article is conceived with perception and cleverly executed.

The humor of "Los médicos y los dolientes" (*El Mosaico*, May 28, 1864) is rather grisly, for the article deals with the helplessness of the sick in the hands of jealous and incompetent doctors and well-meaning but unjudicious relatives and friends. It is not one of Marroquín's best pieces, but it is of interest for its use of such a hoary thesis (Silva and Guarín used it too), and for the fact that Marroquín, even as we today, is more than a little reticent and indirect in his criticism of doctors.

"Mi tintero" (*El Mosaico*, July 16, 1864) was apparently intended to be a medley of type sketches in the tradition of Larra's "Varios caracteres," but it was left unfinished. It is interesting for what Marroquín calls his "estrambótica teoría" that his inkwell contains all the world's great ideas, and, could he but discover the secret of arranging them on paper, he would write great articles of manners.

> ... En lo que más me recreo es en imaginarme que algunas gotas de tinta bien aprovechadas se riegan y se distribuyen sobre hojas de papel en forma de artículos de costumbres llenos a un mismo tiempo de festiva ligereza y de profundas observaciones, de sátira finísima y de sal santafereña (no digo sal ática porque ¡qué diablo! entonces se diria: "en casa del herrero, azadon de palo.").

The article then flays the chronic malcontent who voices the malignant Hispanic conviction that every place else is better than the place he is in, and the bore who asks poets to write casual verse for his friends' saint's days. A curious feature of the article is a series of mock-epic oaths and epithets of classic flavor, like "pedazo de alcornoque," "gaznápiro," "alma de cántaro," "grandísimo avestruz," "mengua de los estólidos," etc.

"¿Quién es el más feliz de los mortales?" (*El Mosaico,* April 30, 1864) argues in a lively manner the whimsical thesis that the wet nurse is the happiest of mortals, presenting in its support an account of a family's helplessness to deny even the most fantastic demands of a simple girl brought in to nurse a delicate baby.

Perhaps the most pleasant of all Marroquín's light satirical articles, at least for the student of languages, is "Los diminutivos." Economic conditions, Marroquín affirms, are partly responsible for the Colombian's exaggerated use of diminutive suffixes. One dare not admit to being prosperous, for the reasons explained in "Contribuciones directas," hence the man of means speaks of his *ahorritos,* his *terrenito,* and his *negocito,* lives in a *casita* worth twenty thousand pesos, and harvests from his *sementerita* an abundant crop which he calls *un poquito de trigo.* "Dios me libre," says the author, "de los que dicen majestuosamente *mis negocios, mi hacienda, mis caballos, mi capital*: a los tales no les fiaria yo mis intereses (quiero decir *mis cortos intereses*)." The diminutive also reduces the pain of certain transactions; for example, the creditor suggests drawing up a *documentito* providing for a *placito* of six or eight years, and the debtor, paying his *realitos,* demands a *recibito.* Authors are no less hypocritical than businessmen, of course. An author will say:

> —Sí, señor: he compuesto una *obrita* y puede ser que en este año.... Y el muy bellaco tiene allá para su capote que su *obrita* es un *obron* que deja eu pañales todas las obras de Chateaubriand.
> —Por ahí he de tener unos *versitos* que hice sobre ese asunto. ... Y el hipocriton, que sabe muy bien donde los tiene y que perece por leérselos a todo el universo, no los daria por la Divina Comedia....

And Marroquín insists that this article, though it cost him a whole night's sleep and went through four drafts, is only an *articulito.* This is first class festive satire, and one of Marroquín's most sparkling articles.

In 1879 Marroquín lectured before a charitable society on the vice of *lujo,* "ostentation," which he considered a threat to the national economy. He said,

> ... El lujo de que trato, el que, como gangrena, corroe y devora nuestra sociedad, es el que consiste en que cada uno pretende colocarse o mantenerse en una categoría social que supone recursos superiores a los que posee.... El antiguo *qué dirán,* cansado de oírse vituperar y maldecir, ha huído de entre nosotros; pero en

lugar suyo ha venido a enseñorearse de las conciencias otra frase: *sería muy feo!*

The lecture was published in *El Zipa*, a literary paper which ran from August, 1877, to December, 1881, and immediately afterward Marroquín started writing himself letters, signed with his old pseudonym P. P. de P., in which he enlarged and illustrated his concept of the evil of *lujo*. These letters, which were also published in *El Zipa*, form a series of coordinated essays on manners unique in Colombian *costumbrismo* for their sustained criticism of a central evil, and with them Marroquín develops into a full-fledged censor of manners.

The first and probably the least important of the series is "Mis nuevas confidencias," dated September 15, 1879, in which the author represents himself as one of five children who jointly inherited their father's 150,000 pesos. He cannot adapt himself to a 30,000 peso scale of living, and, further, society in its demands on him fails to recognize him as only one-fifth of his father, so he resorts ultimately to speculation and ruins himself altogether. The problem was probably not a very general one, the article is too long, and the details of the economic fiasco are repetitious, but the humor is good and its high spot is in the accounts of the author's uncommon expenditures.

Préstamo, con carácter de perpetuidad, a un respetabilísimo amigo de mi familia .... $ 25

Composición de la cañería que debía traer el agua a la *casita* 50

Al maestro Calasancio, para que desempeñara sus herramientas, y pudiera venir a desempeñar su deber concluyendo la obra de la cañería 7

Multa por haber tenido destapada la cañería demasiado tiempo, a causa del empeño de las herramientas 6

Viajes de un comisionado a refrescarles las ideas a deudores olvidadizos 80

Valor de una mula que compré para los viajes de dicho comisionado, considerando que así gastaría menos que en alquileres 110

Gastos para buscar la misma mula luégo que se perdió 15

The title of Marroquín's second letter to himself comes from Cervantes—"Las bodas de Camacho." His nephew Eduardo has saved from his eighty pesos monthly a sum of five hundred pesos to cover the expenses of his marriage and to set himself up in housekeeping. Having rented a suitable house, no small item in itself, his relatives undertake to advise him in furnishing it, and, since they all hold the doctrine of *sería muy feo*, his modest budget is exceeded in no time. Similar extravagance is the keynote of the wedding (in the archbishop's chapel because any lesser locale *sería muy feo*!) and the reception, and the final expenditure is 2,744.40 pesos, half of which, says Marroquín, would have been enough to marry the son of the city's richest merchant. And the futility of it all is illustrated by a conversation between two of the bride's friends a few days later:

—¡Ay! A mí me dieron ganas de llorar. ¿Para qué iría Alicia a casarse con un hombre tan vulgar? ¿Qué casa la que le ha puesto!

—¡Sí, Dios mío! ¡qué miseria! ¡Aquella sala sin alfombra!

—¡Y aquellos espejitos como los que venden los mercachifles!

—Y sin piano. ¡Y qué candelabros y qué todo!

The only result was Eduardo's financial ruin, for within a few months he was trying to sell at discount the furniture which was to have convinced the public of his opulence. The subject of this article has more general interest than that of "Mis nuevas confidencias," and the humor, most of it ironic, is even better. As is customary with Marroquín, the article is logically planned and executed with imagination.

In the third and most effective of the series Marroquín brings his theme to bear on ostentatious funerals. "El entierro de mi compadre (Artículo de requiem)" opens with a general statement that, since death is and is intended to be the most humiliating of all human experiences, the elaborate funeral is the most vulgar of all ostentation. The author then relates his experience in arranging for the funeral of his friend Timoteo, whose widow charged him thus: "Para Timoteo, hay que hacer todo lo mejor que se pueda." His responsibility is shared by a number of self-appointed mourners who insist on many extravagant details even when they are themselves aware of their bad taste, only so that "no se diga que por ahorrar se ha dejado de hacer eso." The author hesitates to buy the most fashionable casket—in the shape of a cigar case—for he knows the family cannot afford it, but his instructions were that "había que gastar lo más que se pudiera." He firmly opposes posting announcements of the funeral in the streets, but they are prepared all the same, with the heading:

¡¡¡EL SEÑOR TIMOTEO N. HA MUERTO!!!

There is extravagance even in the exclamation points.

The church is adorned with three hundred candles, sixty lamps, and eight chemical *infiernitos* that give off a cadaverous blue light. Marroquín achieves a climax of irony by contrasting the sumptuousness of the trappings with the humility of the service:

> Allí, en medio de aquel ostentoso aparato, de aquella pompa con que el orgullo humano se empeña en protestar contra la humillación a que nos sujeta la muerte, y en cubrir con oro los despojos que ella ha dejado como señal de su victoria, se convida a los fieles a la oración.
> ". . . Venid, adoremos a Dios y postrémonos en su presencia; lloremos ante el Señor que nos crió, porque El es el Señor nuestro Dios. . . ."
> Allí, en medio de aquel aparato y de aquella pompa se canta:
> ". . . Entraré en vuestra casa, y con santo temor doblaré las rodillas ante vuestro santuario. . . ."

The climax of folly is the use of two hearses.

> Tras el carro mortuorio en que iba el cadáver, llevaban otro *de respeto* como a fin de que no quedase duda de que se había discurrido para hallar modos de evitar que el entierro fuera a costar poco dinero.
> ¡Vanidad de vanidades!

It would be less vulgar, the author suggests, simply to burn a stack of bank notes.

Marroquín's itemized account of the expenses, which ironically notes that much of that which cost so dearly was imitation—imitation bronze on the casket, etc.—totals to 821 pesos. An additional 522 pesos was spent on mourning clothes. His final observation is: "La función fue hecha en sus tres cuartas partes por miramientos al *sería muy feo*, o lo que es lo mismo, por satisfacer la vanidad de los sobrevivientes." And he concludes with an apology to his deceased friend for having been party to such barbarous extravagance.

This article, which is probably Marroquín's best, covers in a masterful way every aspect of the vain cult of mourning. He achieves strong satirical effect without gratuitous exaggeration, and, though his tone is informal, his purpose is deadly serious.

A later article, called "Si he dejado el piano," deals with *lujo* in a much more frivolous way, after the manner of the earlier satirical pieces.

A guide to the evaluation of Marroquín's *costumbrista* work is found in Daniel Samper Ortega's introduction to his collection of articles by Ricardo Silva (Selección Samper Ortega, Volume XXV). Samper says that Marroquín "fue el más cultivado de los 'mosaicos' y el de mayor valía como escritor." This would seem to be a valid appraisal. Marroquín is effective in a wide range of subjects and treatment. "El domingo por la mañana" is an example of the trivial personal essay which was a favorite vehicle among Colombian *costumbristas*. "Los diminutivos" is a little masterpiece of whimsical observation, and "Vamos a misa al pueblo" is an excellent descriptive *cuadro*. In satire he moves effectively from the frivolous criticism of "La penitencia" to the serious didacticism of his series on *lujo*. He seems to have composed with plan and care—his "Los diminutivos" may really have gone through four drafts, as he claims in jest—for only one of his articles, "Mi tintero," shows the mark of impromptu composition; the others all have a logical plan marked by climactic arrangement and easy transition. The plan of his articles suggests Larra, for he always proceeds from an introductory statement of a general concept or observation to the specific problem at hand, and only such a technique can give a sketch of manners the perspective essential to its consideration as serious literature. Not all of his articles are masterpieces, but most of them are among the best of the genre in Colombia.

That which distinguishes Marroquín above all else is his style, which is rare for its measure and purity. It is free from Americanisms and colloquialisms, always correct, always dignified and at the same time informal. It is marked by a suggestive and unobtrusively erudite vocabulary, a fondness for the delicate pun, and adroit but uncomplicated figures. However, the quality of Marroquín's humor is inconsistent. At best he exemplifies what the Spanish call *humorismo*, a fertile wit most effectively displayed in the irony, following the classic Spanish tradition, of his more serious critical articles, but he is also sometimes guilty, as are most of the *costumbristas*, of stringing *chistes* together unnaturally. When he is funny and nothing else, as in "El domingo por la mañana," he proves that nonsense is not his forte.

In short, Marroquín at his best achieves the ideal he set for himself in "Mi tintero"—"artículos de costumbres llenos a un mismo tiempo de festiva ligereza y de profundas observaciones, de sátira finísma y de sal santafereña." All things considered, he is probably the best of the Colombian *costumbristas*.

GUARÍN

José David Guarín (1830-1890) was a prolific and popular *costumbrista* and a prominent member of the Mosaico. He was born in Quetame, a village some sixty kilometers southeast of

Bogotá, and died in Chiquinquirá. His career included founding and operating a school in Bucaramanga, various political jobs ranging from a consular post in the United States to proofreading the *Diario Oficial,* and collaboration on many important periodicals: *El Mosaico, La Biblioteca de Señoritas, El Iris, El Tiempo, La Pluma,* etc. He wrote principally *costumbrista* and miscellaneous essays, but also has a novel, *Las tres semanas* (Bogotá, 1884), and a short play. His articles, which were usually signed with his second given name or his favorite pseudonym, *El Fisgón,* have been collected several times. The best collection is *Obras* (Bogotá, 1880), with an introduction by Adriano Páez; he is represented by six articles in the Selección Samper Ortega, Volume XXVI.

One of Guarín's earliest articles, "Un día de San Juan en tierra caliente" (*El Mosaico,* June 26, July 2, July 9, 1859), is also one of his most popular. It is an entertaining account, in personal essay form, of the festival of St. John in a rural community where the author is a visitor. He is awakened by a midnight hubbub which his landlady tells him is made by the townspeople on their way to the river to bathe in the blessed water of St. John's Eve. He is prompted to wonder, "Si ésta es la víspera qué será el día!" In the uproar of the following day he is thrown from a borrowed horse, captivated by a *calentanita* in a crowded tavern, and at noon accompanies the merrymakers on a second boisterous excursion to the river. At the river there is bathing, dancing—especially the graceful *bambuco*—dinner, and *aguardiente.*

Guarín's descriptions of people and landscapes are good. His landlady, for example:

> Esta era . . . una vieja ochentona y con más arrugas que pelos tiene un cuero, más sorda que quien no quiere oír; la nariz de pico de águila y la barba puntiaguda estaban tan vecinas, que eran necesarias conjeturas o cálculos matemáticos para adivinar dónde estaría la boca, que era como una cortadura; un colmillo creo que le había quedado para atestiguar que en un tiempo había tenido con qué morder.

Also the *bambuco*:

> ¡Quién pudiera haceros sentir, lectorcitos míos, lo que es un bambuco entonado en las playas de un río por dos voces femeniles, sin más acompañamiento que los tiples. . . . Yo no sé qué calificativo darle a este baile; si airoso, elegante o arrebatador; apenas oye uno su música, quisiera bailar o gritar, y cosa extraña! es triste también el bambuco cuando se quiere. Este aire nacional,

tan antiguo como nosotros, es siempre tan nuevo como el día que está pasando. . . .

He refers at one point to the leaves of the palm "que se dejan mecer a los soplos de la brisa como se mueve el talle de una mujer para hacer un desdén."

Guarín shows a sensitive appreciation for the *fiesta*, its setting, and the participants, and he achieves a pleasing combination of seriousness and humor. It may be true, as Adriano Páez says, that those who read the article when it first appeared nearly died laughing, for the humor is good.

A potboiler called simply "Un artículo de costumbres" (*El Mosaico*, June 4, 1859) is of interest for Guarín's notions about the *costumbrista* craft. He complains about short-sighted criticism: the author has ruined a good subject, the style is rough, the ideas confused, no verisimilitude in the descriptions, even rules of grammar violated (all complaints too frequently justified). He then admonishes a companion who aspires to write manners, "Usted por supuesto habrá leído los modelos de la literatura española, como Larra, Mesonero, Fray Gerundio, etc." The enlightened retort is: "¡Qué gerundio, ni qué supino! ¿Acaso para decir lo que uno está viendo aquí todos los días se necesita de todos esos preliminares . . . ?" (Ironically, in his prologue to Guarín's *Obras*, Adriano Páez accuses Guarín of the same indifference to models.)

"La camisa calentana" (*El Mosaico*, August 20, September 3, 1859) is a *cuadro* of the "hot country" landscape and people near Ibagué. The description of the volcano El Tolima is a good example of Guarín's whimsical impressionism:

> Figúrese usted una gran mole diáfana, brillante, cristalina y trasparente, pero que no sea semejante a la plata pulida ni a los lagos iluminados por la luna, ni al diamante herido por la luz, y de ese conjunto de suavidad y brillantez, de opacidad y luz revista una masa tan enorme que su cúspide vaya hasta las nubes y su base se extienda indefinidamente formando las cordilleras de los Andes que más lejos vuelen a mostrar el Santa Isabel y el Ruiz. Déle usted a ese conjunto, golpes de sombra en las quiebras, puntos casi luminosos en las prominencias, báñele la cúspide con el color rosado más suave, más fino y más delicado que encuentre, pero que no sea el rosicler de la concha, ni lo purpúreo de la rosa, sino esa luz divina de la aurora reflejada sobre la nieve, y tendrá una idea del Tolima.

At a country dance, organized by a group of *ñapangas*, or mestizas, Guarín is impressed by the tasteful simplicity of the *décor* and the beauty of the girls, whom he describes as rhapsodically as the volcano; and here he mentions the *camisa* which gave him his title—"Las camisas con primorosos bordados, vienen dibujando cinturas de mimbre; camisas que intentan pero no pueden ocultar las formas de espaldas y pechos como ideados. . . ." As proof of Ibagué's charm, Guarín concludes by introducing an eccentric young Englishman (he mangles proverbs—"El que ha de morir a oscuras, más vale pájaro en mano") so enthralled with the place and the people that he stretches an intended visit of a week into two months. The whole is a really charming *cuadro*.

"Me voy de Bogotá" (*El Mosaico*, November 26, 1859), a slapstick tale of the calamities which befall a rustic visiting the capital, has little interest or value.

One of Guarín's best and most famous pieces, "Entre usted, que se moja" (*El Mosaico*, January 29, February 5, February 12, 1859), is a *leyenda histórica* about an unlikely love intrigue in the early days of independence. The story is as engaging as the title, but it has little *costumbrista* value.

In "Los cuidados también matan" (*El Mosaico*, March 31, 1859) Guarín carries on the Larra tradition of roasting the *bourgeoisie*. It is an account of a birthday feast during which the well-meaning women of his family oblige him to eat so much of the many delicacies they have prepared that he is put to bed with an attack of fever and vertigo. He is further martyrized by their misguided efforts to diagnose his malady and ease his discomfort; then he dies, ostensibly, and suffers the indignity of hearing the remarks of his alleged friends on his life and character. The article is cleverly written, except for an insipid introduction. He says his family and guests sat down at the table "colmados de esa dulce satisfacción que produce en unos el orgullo de haber convidado, y en otros el de haber sido de los escogidos." One of the ladies present, no longer young and still unmarried, "tenía el *palito*, como solemos decir, o la gracia especial para ponerse *pensamientos* blancos en la cabeza, ya que en ella nadie los había puesto hasta el presente ni aun negros." The humor is good and there are frequent flashes of insight and keen satire.

"El maestro Julián" (*El Mosaico*, April 22, 1865; dated 1862 in the *Obras* collection) is an excellent sketch of a remarkable character. Julián is a jack-of-all-trades who, in a shop no more than twelve feet square, in which he and his wife also live, operates a primary school, does tailoring, barbering, shoemaking, and many another useful service:

¿Necesita [usted] un escrito de los de *ante usted represento y digo*? Déjese de buscar abogado, que le pide un sentido y no le hace cosa que sirva; el maestro sabe todas esas fórmulas tan necesarias que no dicen nada, y sobre todo, le llevará muy poco por su trabajo. Además, allí, y sólo allí pueden hacerle calzones de *tapabalazo* y fundillo, tan escasos hoy; quitan manchas a la ropa de paño que no las tenga; le embolan sus botas con betún fabricado de humo de papel y panela, le remiendan cuanto tenga roto, se comprometen a cuanto usted quiera, y por último, le escriben cartas de amores para cualquier situación en que éstos se encuentren. Y usted ve, señor lector, que un establecimiento de éstos no en todas partes se halla.

The composition of love letters is Julián's most profitable activity—"si es de amores no más, vale un real; si es de amor despechado vale real y medio, y si es de amor correspondido, vale dos reales." There is a touch of pathos when a servant girl enters the shop to contract for a letter to a lover who has abandoned her ("ésas de amor dormido valen más"); the arrangement is made—there will be hearts with arrows and a poem at the end—and the *maestro* dictates the letter to one of his pupils while the other students recite aloud their catechism. The maestro's wife is also talented, especially in the subtle delivery of *billets doux*. In this sketch Guarín makes the most of an excellent subject; however, though the language is racy and humorous, it is also sometimes unintelligible.

"Cuadros mimoplásticos" (1864), though it contains the author's impressions of Bogotá after a three-year absence (presumably enforced by the Mosquera revolution), is interesting primarily for information on the curious theatrical diversion mentioned by Restrepo in his "Una noche en Bogotá" as "estatuas." In the performance seen by Guarín the first tableau is an elaborately symbolic affair with a white horse, a golden chariot, and a laurel-crowned lady representing Colombia. The second has the same motif, altered to show the confusion and strife Colombia was then undergoing. The author leaves at this point. Apparently this function is a commercial venture, but it seems to be staged clandestinely in a house in an outlying district of the city. Guarín says it is "medio secreto" but offers the modesty of the participating ladies as the only reason for the secrecy. There must have been another reason.

One of Guarín's most famous articles, and justly so, is "La docena de pañuelos" (*El Mosaico*, April 2, 1864), ostensibly an account of a business venture, actually a picture of a provincial market. The article is dedicated to Ricardo Silva, from whom the author had bought a dozen bright handkerchiefs for resale in his provincial store. Guarín anticipated a two-hundred per cent profit, but found his Indian customers less susceptible to his salesmanship than expected and he had ultimately to resort to a stratagem to dispose of the merchandise. One of the very effective parts of the piece is a dialogue used to convey the hurly-burly of the store at the height of the trading on market day.

En esto empezó a llenarse la tienda.
—*Abájeme sumercé* un lazo, pero escójamelo.
—Me cambia un franco? Pero buena plata.
—Estos reales *cundinos* no los quieren.
—Cuánto es lo último del pañuelito? volvió a preguntar el mismo indio del principio.
—Cinco reales. Mientras se fué he vendido tres, y han quedado de venir por más para el Córpus.
—Rebájeme *sumercé* y tratamos. Buena plata.
—No puedo. Lleva las cuerdas, o no? Y si no, déjelas.
—No, mi amo, de mí no haga *esconfianza enque* soy indio.
—La bogotana?
—A dos y medio.
—Compra mantequilla?
—No.
—Alcáncela *pa* verla.
—Muy fina y ancha.
—Pero como un colador, dijo la india después de refregarla.
—Un cuartillo de clavo y canela.
—Tome, pero deme cuartillo hecho.
—Lo último? Le llevo media vara.
—Que si hay *piedra contra.*
—No.
—Hay *alimento belisanio?*
—Qué?
—*Alimento belisanio*, de ése que sirve para las *lacras*.
—Linimento veneciano, será.
—Sí, mi amo. Véndame *sumercé* un cuartillo.
—No hay.

Other scenes from the market are handled with equal color and realism. The style and organization of this article seem to indicate greater care and planning than is the custom with Guarín; the result is a decidedly successful blending of the personal essay and the realistic *cuadro*.

A letter to José María Vergara y Vergara is the form of "San Isidro Labrador" (*El Mosaico*, September 17, 1864), which finds Guarín in the unusual role of serious recorder of two curious religious celebrations observed in the provinces. One is the "battle of the Virgin" in the village of Chocontá. The first Sunday in October, Guarín says, the image of the Virgen del Rosario is carried into the plaza, where she becomes the center of a sham battle. Guarín is told that the source of the custom is a battle between Torquemada, the Inquisitor, and the forces of the infidel, in which the day was saved for the faithful when the Virgin was carried on the field.

The other celebration is the primitively beautiful festival of San Isidro, patron of farmers, in the village of Guachetá. A procession of drums, flutes, and dancing Indians bears San Isidro to the plaza where all the tasks of the farmer are performed in his presence.

> En la éra se ejecuta la trilla, haciendo unos indios de yeguas y otros de arrieros, y más adelante un gañán con su púa arrea a dos indios que, uncidos al yugo, aran la tierra. A estos bueyes, que llaman de San Isidro, todos les traen chicha; así es que cuando la función se acaba ya no pueden arar sino de hocicos.

San Isidro is dressed in "sombrero alón prendido por delante a la copa; chaqueta colorada, calzón azul ajustado hasta la rodilla y de ahí para abajo medias y zapatos." Also, the image is equipped with the inevitable yoke of oxen, but "más de cuatro dolores de espaldas tendría el Santo al arar con tales bueyes, pues apenas le daban a la mitad de la espinilla."

Interesting features of the article are the references to the *costumbrista*'s mission and responsibility in reporting and recording such *fiestas*. The descriptions are interesting and adequate though not brilliant.

Political satire is the substance of "Favores de la suerte" (1869), in which Guarín argues that Fortune is not blind, but "ve y ve más que un agiotista." The author is pleased at having got a well-paying government job, "conseguido sin intriguillas, padrinazgos ni bajezas, monedas que hay que pagar para conseguir cualquier cosa en este sentido," but at the end of the month he finds the treasury is bare and his salary uncollectable. Nevertheless he plans a picnic with his family, including his wife's cousins, who "tienen . . . la doble ventaja de ser muchas y muy bonitas," but he is prevented from going by a summons to serve as an election official. He is made president of the election board, reviled for refusing to accept forged ballots, starts a riot by denying the right to vote under a false name, and is scolded by his wife for having got involved in politics. A blind Fortune could not have found him so often in so little time, he maintains. Guarín's humorous style is at its best, and the satire on the miserable state of the democratic processes is effective though jocular.

The satire in "Visitar a los enfermos" (1876) is less jocose. When Don Pablo Pinillos takes to his bed with a pulmonary infection, since his wife wants a doctor and he does not, a folk practitioner is called as a compromise. His fantastic potion is ineffective, of course. Friends and relatives begin to call—"como un tabaco encendido en otro se sucedieron las visitas"—and all of them advise and prescribe for the patient. A French doctor is called and dismissed. One caller spills ammonia on Don Pablo's face and mouth, others burn feathers under his nose. None of a long series of doctors is allowed to treat the patient unmolested.

> Siguieron después los remedios de cualquier médico que llegara y de cuantas personas iban a visitar al enfermo, de tal suerte que al fin vino a ser el campo donde se disputaron la preeminencia los empíricos de todas clases, los curanderos y curanderas, los homeopáticos, hidropáticos, alopáticos, y partidarios de cuantos sistemas se hayan imaginado.

Finally the most famous doctor of Bogotá is summoned and makes the accurate prediction that Don Pablo will die within twenty-four hours.

This article has the most earnest satire in Guarín's work. He sets the tone in the introduction:

> Si yo fuera hombre de alientos escribiría, como M. Eugenio Sué hizo con los pecados capitales, tantas novelas cuantas son las obras de misericordia; pues la manera como suelen comprenderlas y practicarlas ciertas personas, da motivo para ello. Asuntos para emprender la tarea, Dios lo sabe, no me faltarían.

His customary attitude of indulgent raillery is missing, though the piece is not without humor. His subject here is very like that of Marroquín's "Los médicos y los dolientes."

"Mi primer caballo," one of Guarín's most carefully written essays, is a charming account of an incident from the author's childhood. At the age of six or seven, in preparation for the *certámenes* at the close of the school year, Guarín was sent to the tailor by his uncle and guardian to be fitted for a suit made from green billiard-table covering—the fabric was too worn for

the billiard table but too serviceable to be discarded. The impression on the boy was more durable than the suit:
> Algunos facultativos hoy, que fueron condiscípulos míos o colegas, me han tomado como asunto serio de estudio y creen que mi color verdoso no es sino un reflejo solidificado del paño del billar. ¿Pero hasta dónde habrá ejercido su influencia esta circunstancia en mi vida, cuando una vieja que me conoció desde niño y a quien le jugué una pillada, decía con gran formalidad, que no en balde tenía yo el alma verde? Y, ciertamente, ¡en cuántos días la he sentido así ante los recuerdos de mi niñez!

The title of the article comes from a broomstick horse with which the boy was obsessed and which was promised him for distinguishing himself in the school ceremonies. His performance was far from distinguished but his tearful disappointment got him the horse anyway; and he lost it the following day!

This article is only secondarily *costumbrista*, but because of its unusual warmth and sensitivity it represents some of Guarín's best writing. In spite of occasional carelessness of style, there are passages of true artistry and feeling:
> Creo que si la fruta pudiera recordar la flor que le sirvió de cuna, por más que el sol la hubiera dorado con sus calientes rayos, por más que la savia la hubiera colmado de aromoso aliento y suaves carnes, y por más que su hermosura fuera la envidia de sus compañeras y la gala del árbol que la crió, desearía volverse a tan inocente estado. Y no se crea que esto suceda por anhelo de prolongar la vida, no; es porque cuando se piensa en la niñez, la imaginación se complace en revestir ese recuerdo con el cendal de la inocencia, con el ropaje del candor; es porque la conciencia siente el goce inefable de un recuerdo sin remordimientos, y así como el sol al partir dora hasta las últimas colinas que ha dejado atrás, así nuestra alma al acercarse cada día al ocaso de esta vida, vuelve retrospectivamente toda su ternura hacia una edad de tranquilos goces que ya nunca volverá.

The article is marred only by a pseudo-romantic protest against the disillusionment of age and experience.

Reminiscence from childhood is also the substance of "Mi cometa," a kite built by the author with great care and affection and lost on its maiden flight. Again he touches on school life, emphasizing the severity of discipline in his Jesuit school. An interesting passage compares men in public life to kites flown by small boys on a windy Sunday morning; the simile is spun too long and fine, perhaps, but it is vivid. There is genuine excitement in the inaugural flight of the treasured kite, but its ultimate crash in the cemetery is played *fortissimo* for its morbid symbolism.

In "La casa arrendada," an entertaining personal essay, Guarín treats the problem of finding housing for his large family ("veinte personas, entre madre, hermanas, sobrinos, tías, parientes y criados que han nacido y vivido con nosotros"). One house is recommended for its inside water.

> Y esa era la verdad, porque, cuando en posesión del manojo de llaves, que pesaban más que las del Escorial, fuí a ver la casa, caí en la cuenta de que no era de azúcar, puesto que había durado tanto tiempo sin desleírse. A una vara de alto se veía lo verde de la lama, prueba evidente de que tenía agua adentro.

Another is a little unsturdy:

> ... Es una trampa de número cuatro: el más afortunado quedará debajo en el próximo mes de invierno, pues, aunque tiene más puntales y resfuerzos que una ley de elecciones, ella a fuerza de gravitar hacia el centro, dará con su figura en tierra.

Another is not very spacious:

> La del chorro de María Teresa, no tiene más defecto que el que decía Larra de otra, y era tener las paredes muy juntas unas de otras; aquello era un miriñaque, una rejita de confesonario, un agujetero donde no cabía uno ni de punta en una multitud de agujeros que llaman cuartos.

He takes a house finally and moves, commenting: "No en balde decía Franklin que dos mudanzas de una casa a otra equivalen al incendio de una." After spending two weeks putting the house and patio in order the house is sold from under him and the hunt resumes. This is one of Guarín's shortest articles and one of his best. The humor is more spontaneous and better sustained than in any of his other work; the language, in spite of some careless lapses, is swift and compact and rich in ingenious figures and suggestive phrasing. The article scintillates from start to end.

Guarín returns to the character sketch in "Un sabio parroquial," in which he lambasts maliciously irresponsible critics of Colombian literature. His subject is a provincial doctor, pompous, smug, and gross, who passes for a wise man in his community. His opinion is that Colombian authors are at best imitators or translators and he avers that even Jorge Isaacs translated his *María* from a French novel whose name the doctor has forgotten. His view of the *costumbristas* is typical:

> ... Poco o nada tenemos de qué hacer alarde: gentes a quienes se les consiente que escriban sus articulitos porque con algo se han de llenar los periódicos, pero que bien averiguado, ni conocen las costumbres que describen, pero ni siquiera el idioma en que quieren escribir. Rapsodistas que ramonean aquí de Mesonero, allí

de Larra, cuando no traducen de Dickens o toman de algún escritor moderno español. Eso es todo.

The author is able to vindicate the Colombian *literato*, cruelly but justly, by identifying the poets from whom the doctor has plagiarized a poem he reads as his own in public recital. The sketch of the fatuous doctor is elaborately done and rich in detail. As in "Visitar a los enfermos," the satire here has none of Guarín's customary indulgence; it is acid and serious.

In appraising Guarín as a *costumbrista* it is first appropriate to observe that he apparently looked upon himself primarily as an entertainer, a fact which may explain his extensive use of the humorous personal essay; only two or three of the articles considered above have other form. He uses the humorous essay sometimes for satire—about a third of his articles are marked by sustained satire—but more often as a vehicle for description, reminiscence, or the presentation of an unusual or interesting aspect of manners.

As a stylist Guarín's greatest attribute is probably his facility for picturesque, humorous expression, often involving colloquialisms, which lends raciness and even compactness to his writing. He generally avoids the bombast and sheer verbiage which are too common in *costumbrismo*, and, though his manner is extremely intimate, he is never naively nice in his attitude toward his reader. His writing is weighted with allusion, sententious asides, and discerning observations that give it both color and substance. His greatest defect as a stylist is his carelessness in syntax and his apparent indifference to correctness as a virtue (his *fe de errata* in his *Obras* acknowledges the presence of many errors and adds, "Enmiéndelas el lector como a bien lo tenga"), but his style probably gains in vigor and sprightliness from that indifference—if he had tried harder he might not have done so well. He has good descriptive passages, often more impressionistic than literal and sometimes, especially in dealing with people, emphasizing the grotesque. There is, unexpectedly, a sensuous note in his descriptions of women.

One of Guarín's most pleasing characteristics is warmth. In a genre which is inevitably personal to some extent he seems to use more of himself, his enthusiasm, his delight, his winsome good cheer than the form demands, and his work gains immeasurably thereby. This is particularly notable in his nature descriptions, marked by personal lyricism, and his sympathetic portrayal of popular festivals and customs; whereas the standard technique is to remain aloof from the masses, Guarín identifies himself by preference with the people in his *cuadros*. He is also somewhat unusual in that he is not a thrall of the "good old days," rarely lauds the past at the expense of the present, and enjoys a kind of insouciance toward authority, morality, and conventionality.

Almost all of Guarín's work has unassuming charm and shows a fully developed sense of humor, without blind spots. His major purpose was to entertain and his choice of subject, execution, and style are directed successfully to that end, but he believed too that the *costumbrista* had a mission as a chronicler and many of his articles—"Un día de San Juan en tierra caliente," "San Isidro Labrador," "La docena de pañuelos"—certainly have historical value. But whatever his purpose, Guarín rarely wrote an article that cannot be read with pleasure today.

SILVA

Ricardo Silva (1836-1887), father of the pre-modernist poet José Asunción Silva and one of the best-loved Colombian *costumbristas*, was a moderate in politics, a successful businessman, and a lover of Bogotá and its traditions. He wrote his first *cuadro de costumbres* to while away an evening of tedium and was surprised at its reception when published in *El Mosaico*. He was a merchant first and a writer second, without literary ambition or vanity. As an amateur he never wrote under pressure, and he was wont to meditate on his subject and its treatment until he was certain he could do it justice. His sixteen essays on manners, collected in a volume he dedicated to his son (*Artículos de costumbres*, Bogotá, 1883), are his entire literary work. Volume XXV of the Selección Samper Ortega is devoted to him.

Silva's earliest articles are rather trivial personal essays written primarily for humorous effect. The first, which overnight earned him a reputation as a *costumbrista*, is "Un domingo en casa" (*El Mosaico*, November 5, 1859), a record of a frustrated quiet Sunday at home. He has servant trouble, a summons for duty at the district court, an urgent appointment as captain of a company of national guard, visits from boisterous neighbor children, and a formal call from a British couple named Prank, whose lap-dog is attacked by the family hound,

. . . el primer ejemplo que se citará entre nosotros, de que un súbdito de tan respetable nación haya sido mordido por un granadino, sin que el negocio nos haya costado algunos millones de pesos.

There is humor in the article and it is written with moderate skill but the enthusiasm with which it was allegedly received is not wholly credible. However, the impression it created is attested by the two sequels it inspired—Crisóstomo Osorio's "Un domingo fuera de casa," and José Joaquín Borda's "Un domingo ni dentro ni fuera de casa."

"El portón de casa" (*El Mosaico*, December 22, 1860) is very like "Un domingo en casa." This time the author seeks quiet at home to prepare a number of *El Mosaico* for which he is guest editor and is thwarted by vendors who knock incessantly at the door. He participates in a grotesque pursuit of an escaped monkey, and the day's mishaps are climaxed when a fugitive bull crashes through his front door. Whereas "Un domingo en casa" has value as a picture of a Colombian household, this article loses touch with reality altogether.

"Ponga usted tienda" (*El Mosaico*, April 9, 1864) is a reply to Guarín's "La docena de pañuelos." The two appeared in successive numbers of *El Mosaico* and are found together in the *Museo de cuadros de costumbres*. In the latter article Guarín had implied that Silva drove a hard bargain in his business dealings with Guarín. Silva replies with an account of his own vicissitudes as a merchant. In this first venture he was duped into buying, without inventory, an unsaleable stock which he finally disposed of by raffle. He was ruined a second time by a revolution. Now the eternal *tertulia* in his store, the chronic bane of the Bogotá shopkeeper, threatens his prosperity.

> ... Mi tienda es el lugar de cita para todos, y el mostrador la tribuna que ocupan constantemente los oradores amigos míos.
>
> En mi tienda se firman todas las representaciones y manifestaciones de gratitud. En ella se recogen bajo mi responsabilidad, las contribuciones para los bailes, banquetes, entradas triunfales, etc., etc.
>
> En la puerta se paran los que no caben dentro, y allí se leen los boletines, hojas sueltas y mensajes.
>
> En mi tienda se reforma todos los días el sistema de gobierno, se analizan las costumbres, se cuentan los últimos chistes y se leen lindísimas producciones literarias.

The conclusion is that Guarín cannot complain of his treatment, for Silva is much worse off than he. The Guarín article has a good deal more color and movement, and even an element of suspense. Silva comes off second best.

The above articles represent Silva's apprenticeship in manners. They treat trivial subjects and have little serious intent—he is neither painting for posterity nor correcting his contemporaries. Their humor, which is pale today, was apparently effective, for some of these articles enjoyed more than average popularity. In later articles Silva either abandons or deepens the personal essay technique and writes with more maturity, depicting scenes and characters that reflect manners more significantly. He even ventures, not always gracefully, into satire.

"Tres visitas" is inspired by Vergara y Vergara's *cuadro*, "El lenguaje de las casas," in which Vergara describes houses representing three periods in Bogotá history—the colonial era, in which the city was known as Santafé, the revolutionary years when the capital was called Santafé de Bogotá, and the contemporary period. Silva accepts Vergara's challenge to sketch the inhabitants of the three houses as he saw them during a Sunday of visiting.

Don Pedro Antonio de Rivera, great-grandson of the builder of the Santafé house, is a man now old, embittered, and resentful of change. But the old man has charm, and Silva leaves with a pleasant impression of his frankness and sense of humor.

In the second house Silva finds a widow of agile tongue and immobilized mind, living with two daughters of forty-odd years whom she calls and treats as *niñas*. Silva escapes from the house eagerly "cansado de sufrir las necedades de aquella mamita y de presenciar el martirio de sus pobres hijas."

Silva's last visit is to the "linda casita de Bogotá," the house Vergara had characterized with the garbled quotation "Fragility, thy name is *extranjero*." The owner, Señor Doronzoro, no less alien than the house, assures Silva that since he has not been in Europe he cannot possibly know "la buena vida," and shows him an album of mementos from the great people he has met in London, Paris, and "su amada Italia." He had even known Lincoln's assasin, a "mozo lleno de *esprit* y de energía." In a rapture of enthusiasm Doronzoro rushes to the piano and "cruelly executes" a selection from Verdi, a purgative that enables him temporarily to act as a Colombian. Then, says Silva, "Yo me retiré . . . agradecido de Verdi que con sus notas delicadas supo corregir por el momento a mi amigo Doronzoro."

In his conclusion, Silva wisely suggests that he and Vergara should include a fourth house, "la casa completa de Bogotá," in which traditional and modern, native and foreign, are brought together in good taste. There are many of them, he says.

This sketch is a worthy complement to Vergara's. The inhabitants of the houses are characterized succinctly and vividly, primarily through skillful use of dialogue.

"Mi familia viajando" is Silva's contribution to the numerous lot of articles—Groot's "Nos fuimos a Ubaque" was apparently the first—dealing with a family excursion to the country. Silva's effort is amusing but undistinguished except for a succinct recapitulation in conclusion:

Hicimos lo siguiente:

... Vestirnos como en la ciudad para recibir las las numerosas visitas. ...

Jugar en el día al volante en el corredor, y de noche, con nuestros amigos, lotería o juegos de prendas hasta que nos dormíamos sobre los carteles, o cumpliendo alguna penitencia como ésta:

"Si es hombre que haga un ramo de flores y lo dedique con verso, y si es señora, que haga un favor y un disfavor."

Comer peor que en Bogotá, y con mil afanes y molestias para mi prima, víctima infeliz que en los veinte días no tuvo uno que no fuera de angustias por atender a los convidados. ...

Carecer de carbón, de agua limpia y de buen pan. ...

Coger moras entre el bosque, espinándonos en la operación las manos. ...

Y por fin de fines, regresar a Bogotá enfermos, flacos, quemados y feos, todo por consecuencia de haber pasado unos días en el campo inmediato a la ciudad.

Silva's best article is "El niño Agapito," a character sketch of the Bogotá *pícaro* who represents the advanced stage of development of the "Chino de Bogotá," the colorful urchin described by Vergara y Vergara. These are Agapito's qualities and station:

Pertenece a la dinastía de las cocineras; es una variedad de aquella familia, y no conoció a sus difuntos padres.

Patojo de profesión, fuerte en *chócolo* y *golosa*, y doctor en ambos modos de robar pañuelos, llevó a cabo, en sus primeros años, mil pillerías que quedaron siempre cubiertas por el "tenebroso velo del anónimo."

Cuña de la barra del Senado en los días de borrasca política, centinela peligroso de los templos o del teatro, apedreador de primera fuerza, caudillo de los silbadores en los fuegos artificiales de las octavas de barrio, campanero insigne, acompañante de los heridos y de los animales raros que traen a la ciudad, es además la burlona plaga de los forasteros ecuestres que hacen figura ridícula, y el guía de los incautos negociantes de provincia que vienen por primera vez a Bogotá.

El *niño Agapito* conoce a todo el mundo en la ciudad, y es grande y buen amigo de las aguadoras y de los mozos de cordel. Es además el eco que lleva a las tabernas lejanas, ya la noticia del último suceso, ya el resumen del bando sobre monedas o sobre aseo, expedido por el nuevo Alcalde del Distrito, y no solamente es inofensivo en el círculo de sus relaciones, sino que es útil a cada paso. En efecto, él es quien arma la trampa de "número cuatro" en la chichería predilecta, hace la casa para el mico, le enseña picardías a la lora y construye el palomar en el corral de la habitación de su madrina. Acompaña al Santísimo hasta el tugurio del infeliz, llevando la campana o el farol que le fué encomendado por el sacristán, arregla el pesebre con montañas de laurel, conchas y casa de cartón en la tienda del maestro zapatero, quema los triquitraques, mueve los títeres y toca la pandereta en las hirvientes y ruidosas francachelas de Noche-buena y aguinaldos.

El *niño Agapito* es el conductor de la cometa, o de los niños de la familia del obrero, conocido suyo, que va el domingo a "La Peña" o al "Río del Arzobispo," y por regla general figura siempre entre los ayudantes de toda empresa de arrabal relacionada con sus amigos.

Society is deprived of Agapito's multifaceted indispensability when he is forcibly recruited into the army, but he soon deceives his sergeant and deserts, taking refuge in a monastery where he immediately makes himself beloved for his ebullient humor.

—Cómo *sa vatil tré bien mister?* le decía, un día en la oscuridad del zarzo del convento, a un *armazón* de Júdas, haciéndole una cortesía.

—*Ciubdadanos* ratones, por qué *os juis!* exclamó en tono marcial al sentir ruido entre los trastajos que movía.

When the war is over Agapito leaves the monastery as abruptly as he had the army and rejoins the latter, spending several glorious days telling spurious battle stories and selling counterfeit war souvenirs in the taverns of Bogotá. Stripped of his military pomp, Agapito becomes a street vendor (a notice on his box of merchandise reads "La tertulia me perjudica. No fío"), and soon is owner of a modest store in the "Calle Real." During the Independence Day *fiestas* he takes an unprofitable flier at operating a gaming table and proposes marriage to his childhood friend *Duviges* (Eduvigis). Ultimately he becomes a successful wholesaler in pottery and is no longer recognizable as "ese conjunto simpático de malicia y de ignorancia, de travesura y de gracia, ligero, activo, servicial y decidor ingenioso" that was *el niño* Agapito.

"El niño Agapito" is by all standards a superior article, a colorful, lively portrait which richly reflects the subject's environment. Agapito is a garrulous, ubiquitous, roguishly independent figure realistically portrayed through description, incident, and dialogue, a character of rare sprightliness sketched with real skill.

In "La cruz del matrimonio" Silva attempts to demonstrate the ignoble thesis that the happiness of a family has been destroyed by the ignorance, sloth, and volatility of its five servants —cook, laundress, nursemaid, "criada de adentro," and houseman. The humor and dialogue are good, but the chief value of the article is its statement of the functions of the servants and their masters' complete dependence on them.

A third group of Silva's articles, those of the last years of his life, are characterized by greater length, interest in minute detail, and nostalgia. One of them is his best satirical piece, "Vaya usted a una junta," in which he ridicules the plethora of committees, commissions, and councils devised by the *bogotano*. Dictionary definition notwithstanding, he says, in Colombia a *junta* "es una reunión de personas que no se reunen," and they are formed because

> así como entre las mercancías tenemos "tela para camisa" y "género para sábanas," hay en los miembros de nuestra sociedad "tela para Juntas" y "género para Secretarios y Tesoreros de las Juntas."

The author is pompously summoned by one Pascual Cordero to attend "una Junta que tendrá lugar para tratar en ella algunos asuntos de alta importancia en la presente situación." The meeting, attended by fourteen of the fifty-two invited, opens two hours late with a well-rehearsed speech by Don Pascual which gives no hint of the *junta*'s purpose. Thereafter the following business is transacted: it is moved that an executive board be elected, then moved that the election be left for the next meeting; it is moved that Don Pascual be provisional president; Don Pascual accepts with more alacrity than modesty. The author impertinently inquires about the purpose of the meeting, learns it is to found an opposition newspaper. One of the members believes Don Pascual's views on the government are offensive to his wife's sister's husband. Names for the *junta* and its paper are offered and rejected. Don Pascual is named editor of the non-existent paper at two hundred non-existent pesos monthly. Eleven shares of stock in the paper are pledged at one hundred and fifty pesos. Committees are named. The meeting adjourns at one o'clock.

The result is this:

> Nueve meses después, los Estatutos y el Reglamento están aún en la mente de los comisionados, el presupuesto en borrador, los ciento cincuenta pesos por acción, en poder de los accionistas, el periódico esperando las manifestaciones espontáneas de la opinión en favor del candidato de la oposición, y D. Pascual la reunión de la segunda Junta que debe elegir la comisión de mesa y aprobar o improbar los trabajos de las comisiones.

This article is one of Silva's best. The satire, neither too exaggerated nor too caustic, is witty and penetrating. Many of the types of citizens who make up the "tela para Juntas" are deftly sketched, and the air of confusion which, combined with utter egoism, makes the *junta* worse than futile is clearly conveyed through skillful dialogue. It is the only article in which Silva probes below external manners into the fundamental character of his countrymen.

"Un remiendito" exposes the hazards of remodeling an old house. Silva uses the experience of Doña Pilar Tapias, who, urged by her *compadre* Don Serafín, undertakes some minor improvements on her house, to demonstrate that "un remiendito, pues, es la rueda dentada de una gran máquina de limpiar el bolsillo." One minor repair led to another and eventually to the renovation of the entire building—"Con unos dos mil fuertes ... bien gastaditos," said Serafín, "podría hacerse un palacio." The result was tragedy. The façade of the building split down the middle, the municipality condemned it, Doña Pilar went heavily into debt, a neighbor won a suit for damages, the work was interrupted by a revolution, and Doña Pilar died before it was resumed. Silva shows in this piece a new interest in detail, the ironic humor is fine, technical terminology is used to good comic effect, and there is life in the characters and speech of Don Serafín and the maestro in charge of the construction.

"Las llavecitas" is a sweeping condemnation of the passion for imported modernity about which Vergara wrote in "El lenguaje de las casas" and "Las tres tazas." Silva's complaint is:

> Vino el progreso moderno que todo lo ha invadido llevándose de paso los rasgos característicos de nuestras sencillas costumbres; dejándonos en cambio sin fisonomía propia, y haciendo de nuestro modo de ser una especie de colcha de retazos de diferentes nacionali-

dades, como las nuestras de zaraza que cubren las camas de algunos pobres.

The "llavecitas" of the title are little French keys that have replaced the two gigantic keys to the ponderous cabinets in the pantry of the traditional Bogotá house. Silva uses them as a symbolic hook on which to hang a series of rhetorical questions —"¿Dónde están nuestra sencillez en las maneras y en el vestir, la cordialidad y el buen humor que nos caracterizaban?"— through which he reviews the richness of Colombian tradition in order to contrast it with the heritage being prepared for future generations. His descendants, he says,

> ... Tomarán el té, el aristocrático té, huésped extranjero, servido en tetera de Elklington con coladorcito de alambre dorado; endulzado con azúcar de remolacha, al cual le hace una vénia la dorada vinajera resplandeciente, para servirle unas gotas de leche condensada y preparada por Lanman y Kemp, y ante cuya majestad apenas se permite presentar sus doradas, azuladas y aromáticas espumas, servido en diminutas tazas y en alarmante minoría, el chocolate vergonzante, proscrito vulgar, noble arruinado, delicia un día de los que fueron, y hazme-reír hoy de la Charlotte Russe, de los barquillos de Morton, de las galleticas de agengibre de Huntley, del *plumpuding*, de los *sandwiches*, de los *rice-cakes*, de la *crème de almendras amargas* y de los demás cortesanos extranjeros, acompañantes obligados de aquel invasor chino, hijo adoptivo de la Gran Bretaña, y que en segundas o terceras nupcias o decocciones es apurado con aparente placer por las víctimas del buen tono.

Perhaps the length of this breathless sentence is a thermometer of Silva's passion. No Anglophile he. Here is a violence seen nowhere else in Silva's work, and an unsuspected capacity for invective. For a few pages he becomes a first rate satirist. Unfortunately, here also is the addiction to the past which gives an effete odor of lavender to much of Colombian *costumbrismo*. The latter part of the article is a conventional narrative treatment of the distress caused by the "llavecitas" in the modern household. Silva touches, incidentally, in addition to the foreign and the modern, the *lujo* theme of Marroquín.

The same themes—foreignism, modernism, and ostentation—are the basis of "Un año en la corte," a long, novelistic article about a provincial family of means which is nearly ruined by involvement in the elegant social circle of the capital. The father summarizes the experience, addressing the family:

> ... Extraño a tales costumbres, que no fueron las patriarcales que conocí en Bogotá; sin tener idea de semejante lujo en una

ciudad pobre como ésta, yo mismo quise descansar y que disfrutaran ustedes, con un poco más de gesto, de las ventajas de la capital. Pero dónde, ni trastornado de la cabeza, pude figurarme que vivir en una jaula de canarios, bailar unas polkas, hacer y recibir unas visitas, y conocer el Congreso y el Salto de Tequendama, pudiera costarle a uno una gran parte de su fortuna en pocos meses? . . . Pues un esfuercito más en materia de goces en Bogotá, y quedamos como pepas de guama.

This recalls the lament of Quintín, in "Fiestas," written forty years earlier.

The article is rather like a mosaic of *cuadros* on many subjects, enhanced by descriptions of houses, furniture, and costumes, sprightly folk dialogue, and the comic effect of the impact of "refinement" on the provincial family and vice versa. One of Silva's most ambitious articles, it is a successful combination of local color, interesting narrative, artistic description, and effective criticism.

"La niña Salomé," Silva's last article, is a companion piece to "El niño Agapito." Salomé, daughter of a cook, spent much of her childhood with her godmother, the proprietress of a *chichería*, who saw that the girl got at least a little schooling. As a child she was as mischievous as she was intelligent and industrious.

Salomé pronunciaba llena de gracia, la *resunta* en la apertura de los certámenes, y a la cabeza de las *escuelantas*; cantaba el himno a la Virgen el día de la repartición de los premios; ayudaba a su madrina a vestir de flores la cruz de Mayo, y a preparar los floreros, a hacer las ensaladas, y a poner la mesa para las cenas que los *"señores decentes"* solían encargar. Recitaba graciosos versos populares, sabía como se llamaban algunas *cachacas*, quemaba triquitraques sobre el gato dormido, montaba en las inofensivas burras transeuntes y era el mismo diablito del barrio, tormento de su mamá y encanto de su madrina que la *consentía*, y de los parroquianos que la admiraban y que le regalaban cuartillos por "oírle el pico."

At fifteen Salomé went into service and quickly became "el ojo derecho" of the mistress and the companion of her two daughters. When one of the daughters married, Salomé went to the new home and soon married the husband's manservant, Feliciano, whom she followed into the field during the inevitable revolution. Feliciano was killed in action and Salomé returned to Bogotá to care for her blind, infirm godmother. "La niña Salomé" is a worthy companion to "El niño Agapito" in the gallery of Bogotá types, but, although Salomé is a lovable mixture of mischief, utility, and devotion, Silva does not manage to give her the same degree of color and picaresque charm he gave Agapito. About half of the sketch is detailed description of Salomé's hovel and the *chichería*, which, regardless of its value as description, is not pertinent to the character of the girl. Nevertheless, "La niña Salomé" is one of Silva's better articles and a character sketch that has few peers in the literature of the time.

Silva's development as a writer can be clearly followed in the chronology of his articles. His earliest work is trivia, written as much for his own amusement as for any other reason, and its dominant feature is a naive humor not as funny today as it may have been a hundred years ago. The first of his articles to show genuine promise is "Tres visitas," in which he displays the nascent ability at character portrayal which later becomes his most conspicuous talent. The essays that follow show a greater concern and perception for the portrayal of manners and he takes a critical attitude which produces two or three pieces of satirical value. No longer content merely to amuse, he makes a creditable effort to correct as well. His later articles become longer and more novelistic and he begins to indulge a passion for descriptive detail. Some of them, "La niña Salomé," for example, are top-heavy with lavish description. Unfortunately, his talent for description is not great, for, although his pictures are rich in detail, they are purely photographic and lifeless. In general, however, his work improves with the years; his style becomes smoother, he becomes more observant and reflective, and more original.

As a stylist Silva is not outstanding. At the outset his manner is wholly unembellished, but as he gains experience his writing becomes more suggestive and he uses an occasional figure of speech. In his later work there is a note of irony which is the more effective for being unexpected, and at dialogue he has more than average skill.

On two counts Silva deserves the highest rating. One is organization and development of his subjects. He apparently planned carefully, for each of his articles begins with a statement of the problem or subject in the abstract, proceeds to an illustrative narrative, and concludes with a proper summation, all with a minimum of digression and no confusion. His consistency is rare in a genre characterized by improvisation. His other claim to distinction is his excellence in the character sketch. His reputation rests primarily on "El niño Agapito," a masterpiece for its completeness, its interest, and the effectiveness of its reflection of *milieu*. "La niña Salomé" is less excellent but still a credit to a first-rate talent.

DÍAZ

Eugenio Díaz (1804-1865) is a *costumbrista* in a class by himself. He was a man of the people who knew peasant customs because they were his customs, not from distant and detached observation. He was born in the little town of Soacha on the Bogotá *sabana*, attended secondary school for a brief time, then worked as a farmer, tobacco grower, and in the sugar mills. He was often the overseer on the estate of an absentee landlord, and sometimes worked his own land. When he was over fifty he came to Bogotá to seek a means of publishing some of the articles he had worked out during his idle hours, and his meeting with Vergara y Vergara resulted in the founding of *El Mosaico*. In addition to many articles, he is the author of three novels: *Manuela*, which first appeared in 1866 in Vergara's *Museo de cuadros de costumbres*, *Los aguinaldos en Chapinero*, and *El rejo de enlazar* (both Bogotá, 1875). Some of his articles, as well as some chapters from *Manuela*, appear in Volume XXIII of the Selección Samper Ortega.

"El caney del Totumo" (*El Mosaico*, April 14, April 21, 1860) is concerned with the plight of the tobacco grower who must sell his crop to the landowner at one-fourth its value, buy only in the owner's store, and meekly suffer indignity and indecency. Methods of raising tobacco are described, sometimes awkwardly, and the dialogue is realistic, but in general the article is artistically naive. It is effective propaganda for a law to enforce the free sale of tobacco, which is its primary aim.

Mistreatment of the peasant is also the burden of "María Ticince, o los pescadores del Funza" (*El Mosaico*, November 10, 1860), which is more short story than *cuadro*. Denied the right to fish, a peasant father is driven by his family's hunger to put out his nets surreptitiously by night; his raft capsizes and his daughter, María Ticince, the heroine of the piece, is drowned. The characters are not at all real, and, in spite of explicit intentions to the contrary, they are over-idealized. The pathos is too heavy, and the doctrine obvious: "La tumba fué el único atributo de *igualdad* para María; la *fraternidad* fué tal como se ejerce con los pobres de la Nueva Granada; los beneficios de la *libertad*, su historia los manifiesta."

Díaz the crusader is also seen in two articles about the crude method of threshing wheat on the Bogotá *sabana*. The first, "El trilladero de la hacienda de Chingatá," is interesting for a naively detailed explanation of the threshing system by the owner of the *hacienda*:

> Se hacen correr las yeguas en esa era o trilladero que, como usted ve, es un patio practicado en la dehesa, de doce varas de diámetro y cercado por estantillos amarrados con bejuco: en ese estrecho circo se hacen volver los animales y se les da rejo sin misericordia; unos caen, otros se lastiman, otros se raspan las piernas, otros se malogran; pero se trilla, que es lo que importa.

In the other article, "El trilladero del Vinculo" (*El Mosaico*, February 20, 1864), the author's concern again is for the horses, though he also comments on the poor rations allowed the laborers. The feature of the piece is a curious letter written by an overseer to congratulate his master on the purchase of a threshing machine. The letter is either incredibly sentimental or remarkably subtle in its irony.

> Mi muy apreciado amo de mi vida. Pues yo sé que su merced ha montado una imprenta de trillar, y como soy mayordomo por la misericordia de Dios, yo sé todas las aflicciones de las yeguas y las grandes esclavitudes en que viven en un tiempo en que se ha libertado los negros, y los indios, y los padres de los conventos, y los cosecheros del tabaco, y por esto se me hacía muy duro que las madres yeguas no se libertaran, pero sumerced se ha hecho el libertador y ha plantado la imprenta de trillar en las tierras del amo don Raimundo Santamaría, que Dios guarde, y con la indormia que les ha puesto en los ojos a todos los amos de esta sabana, quedan ya libertadas las yeguas lo mismo que estamos todos los granadinos desde que nos libertó el amo Bolívar de los chapetones. Pues yo paso por en medio de estos cuatro borrones, a darle las gracias debidas a sumerced a nombre de toda esta sabana que desde el año de diez no habían podido montarse todavía una imprenta de trillar, aunque mi amo me dijo que un R. padre había traído desde el tiempo de los amos virreyes una máquina de ensuciar papel ... y todas las yeguas de la sabana deben dar a sumerced las gracias puestas de rodillas si son agradecidas con su libertador, y no harán mucho, y el gobierno debe mandarle poner su retrato en el cabildo del estrito [*sic*] de Soacha, y con esto mande sumerced con toda satisfacción a su humilde mayordomo, q. s. m. b.
>
> Juan Antonio Sarmiento
de nada más.

In these articles the only literary refinement that Díaz allows himself is irony, which he uses frequently and not always lightly—the United States is "la república modelo, inventora y propagadora de la ley de Linch." He reports first hand on the manners of the *campo* and the *campesino* with a wealth of authenticating detail, and his championship of the down-trodden, man or beast, is in all ways admirable, but his methods are too naive and awkward to interest any but the most enthusiastic primitivist.

Perhaps Díaz' greatest contribution to literary *costumbrismo* was the invention of a motto which other *costumbristas* took eagerly and hopefully to their hearts: "Los cuadros de costumbres no se inventan; se copian."

CARRASQUILLA

Ricardo Carrasquilla (1827-1886), born in the Cauca valley but long a resident of Bogotá, was one of the original members of the Mosaico and a founding editor of its journal. Self-educated, he devoted most of his life to teaching, and was a champion of modern pedagogical methods. His literary renown is owed mostly to his festive verse written for such papers as *El Album, El Porvenir, La Biblioteca de Señoritas,* and *El Mosaico,* though he acquired some fame as a Catholic apologist for his *Sofismas anticatólicos vistos con microscopio* (Bogotá, 1880), an unconnected series of analogical gymnastics more ingenious than penetrating.

Carrasquilla's essays on manners are not numerous, and some of them only skirt the edges of the genre, but they are sometimes witty and imaginative. "Yo y el diablo" reports a conversation with the devil, "un sujeto rechoncho, con anteojos verdes y embozado en una de esas largas capas de que quedan ya tan pocos ejemplares." The first part is questions by the devil calculated to tempt the author to fleshly pleasure and the author's somewhat petulant answers—he cannot own a horse because friends would borrow it, or rent a box at the theater because there is nothing to see there, etc. The article comes alive only at the end when the author questions the devil. On drunkenness the evil one says:

> —Ha hecho notables progresos: la última vez que vine a Bogotá los borrachos se ocultaban en sus casas porque aún tenían un resto de pudor; pero hoy hacen alarde de su embriaguez, paseándose a la luz del sol en los sitios más públicos de la ciudad.

On Bogotá women:
> —Las hay de dos clases: unas que conservan las antiguas costumbres y que en mi sentir son abominables; y otras que por haberse educado en la escuela de mis novelistas franceses, han llegado al más alto grado de perfección, y saben tanto, que muchas veces se han atrevido a darme lecciones, haciéndome ruborizar de mi ignorancia.

The devil departs with a cheery "Hágame el favor de ponerme a los pies de la señora," and the author replies, "Con muchísimo gusto." The article relies too much on the obvious sulphurous jokes about the devil, but the last part is clever.

Carrasquilla's "Destino irrevocable" is a trivial article on the same theme as Vergara's "El último Abencerraje"—the difficulty of finding and keeping a good horse—and has little to recommend it.

"Un jurado," which first appeared in *El Papel Periódico Ilustrado*, is a complaint about jury duty and a satire of the processes of law. A jury composed of the author, a dandy, an old soldier, a barber, and a usurer considers the case of an Indian charged with the theft of a cow and comes to the remarkable verdict that the crime was not committed and the Indian is guilty! There is less peevishness and more real satire here, but Carrasquilla's concern seems mostly for his personal inconvenience and not at all for the miserable creature "judged" by such a haphazard court of law.

A gay article called "Un álbum" (*El Mosaico*, June 4, 1864) recounts the author's problems in writing a poem for the memory book of a lady he had never seen. He first writes of her "ardientes ojos" and "blanda sonrisa," calling her also "fúljida mariposa," only to learn that she is one-eyed, toothless, and weighs four hundred pounds. He gives up an acrostic to her virtue on being informed it is questionable. In desperation he pastes in an engraving of Saint Vincent de Paul succoring foundlings in the streets of Paris; he learns too late that the recipient has herself produced foundlings. The subject again is trivial, but the article is a valid though superficial reflection of manners. Judging from the number of poems in *El Mosaico* headed "En el album de la señorita ....," every lady of the time had a book in which she collected laudatory or sentimental verse by every *literato* she could snare, and apparently some poets took this genre quite seriously.

Carrasquilla's best articles are "Lo que va de ayer a hoy"

and "El tiempo vale dinero," both of which first were published in *El Mosaico*. The first contrasts education in the author's childhood, presumably about 1835, with that of the 1860's. The first part seems more valuable, for Carrasquilla writes with great vividness of his own student life. He says that he always crossed himself three times before entering the school and his description of it explains why:

> El local de la escuela constaba de . . . una sala estrecha, ahumada, oscura, y tan húmeda, que la pared estaba cubierta hasta la altura de un metro, de una lama verde que producía un olor sumamente desagradable. Una antigua mesa de cedro, una silla de brazos en cuyo espaldar había un toro y un toreador de medio relieve; cuatro bancas durísimas y un largo poyo de adobe eran los únicos muebles que adornaban aquella lúgubre habitación.

Over the teacher's chair, along with the dunce's cap and the rod, was the inevitable motto:

> LA LETRA CON SANGRE DENTRA
> Y LA LABOR CON DOLOR

The school day began with an hour of studying aloud, continued with a half hour of recitation followed by the ceremonial punishment of those who performed unsatisfactorily. A writing lesson and more punishment preceded lunch. After the afternoon session, which followed a similar schedule, the boys retired to the Huerta de Jaime for the pugilistic settlement of the day's disputes.

The second part of the article describes the school the author's nephew now attends. The pupils are dressed and act like gentlemen and study diligently in a comfortable environment, and the dunce's cap and the rod are in the school museum. The article ends with a curious debate in verse, the conclusion of which seems to be that there are virtues in both the old and the new systems. The first part of the piece, at least, stands as a creditable contribution to the chronicle of Colombian manners. This is the essay to which Marroquín appended his "Al señor Ricardo Carrasquilla."

"El tiempo vale dinero" (*El Mosaico*, July 2, 1864) may be the most successful purely humorous article in Colombian *costumbrismo*. In this happy century, Carrasquilla says, it has been discovered that spirit is nothing and matter is everything, and, since time is worth money, time must be saved. Hence, the age of compendium is at hand—the railroad is the compendium of the mule, a bank note the compendium of a stack of gold, etc.—but literature is lagging behind. What does one learn from four volumes of Colombian history except that

> Bolívar tumbó a los godos,
> Y desde ese infausto día
> Por un tirano que había
> Se hicieron tiranos todos?

If *Paul et Virginie* is remarkable for its simplicity, reasons Carrasquilla, it would be even better if further simplified:

> Dos niños juntos se criaron,
> Por supuesto se quisieron;
> Mas luego los separaron,
> Y de dolor se murieron.

Confronted with the failure of literature to keep pace with progress, Carrasquilla has invented, to the eternal glory of Colombia and Carrasquilla, he says, *la literatura homeopática*,[2] which he defines as follows:

> ... Consiste en sacar la quinta esencia de todas las obras maestras, siendo de advertir que aun las más románticas y venenosas vienen a ser inofensivas por la extremada pequeñez de la dosis.

He then presents a dozen works of literature which he has subjected to his epitomizing process. Some of them are:

LA ODISEA
> Hizo Ulises un gran viaje
> Y padeció tanto afán
> Como el que va en mal bagaje
> De Bogotá a Popayán.

EL CONDE DE MONTECRISTO
> Fue Dantés un majadero
> Que por quererse vengar,
> Se privó de disfrutar
> En calma de su dinero.

LOS MISTERIOS DE PARIS
> El zar goza de su imperio,
> El conde de su condado,
> Y el pobre vive *fregado*,
> En lo cual no hallo misterio.

LA ENEIDA
> Eneas, quizá impelido
> Por un destino fatal,
> Dejó abandonada a Dido,

---

[2] The controversy which began with the announcement by Friedrich Hahnemann (1755-1843) of the homeopathic system of therapeutics apparently left a considerable impression on Colombians, for the *costumbristas* often mention the division of opinion, among doctors and laymen, with regard to homeopathy and allopathy. Carrasquilla uses the medical term particularly aptly here, for it connotes not only smallness but relative ineffectuality.

> Y en mi concepto hizo mal.
> COMPENDIO DE TODAS LAS ANACREÓNTICAS
> Mientras el tiempo veloz
> Nos roba, Juana, la dicha,
> Dáme un cuartillo de chicha,
> Papas chorreadas y arroz.

Carrasquilla has two other schemes for modernizing literature. One is particularly remarkable because the twentieth century has proved it wholly practical—microphotography. By ingenious but simple means, he says, the entire works of Voltaire, el Tostado, Lope de Vega, and José María Samper could be so reduced in volume they could be kept in a cigar box. Also, writers might emulate the romantics by using dotted lines (*puntos suspensivos*) to abstract what they do not know how to, do not want to, or are unable to say.

> Concluyo, pues, compendiando en dos renglones de puntos suspensivos
>
> > Mis grandes y profundos pensamientos,
> > Mi vasta erudición y mis talentos.
> > . . . .
> > . . . .

This is an extraordinary article for a number of reasons. First, it is a delicate satire, written with the best of humor—Carrasquilla seems to be laughing at himself and his capricious schemes for improving literature, but he is also protesting against a growing indifference to literature. Second, some of his epitomes of literature are gems in their own right. Third, such delightful whimsy and understatement are rare in Latin American authors. And fourth, Carrasquilla seems to have invented both microphotography and the *Reader's Digest*!

These six articles apparently are all of Carrasquilla's *costumbrista* production. Except for "El tiempo vale dinero" his work is hardly better than average. There is a satirical element in all of his articles, but most of his satire is too superficial and too querulous to be impressive, and his humor, which at best is very good, is generally conventional. A unique aspect of his style is his penchant for mixing prose and verse; he often concludes a sentence with a couplet or a quatrain as though unable to resist the urge to rhyme. This habit is usually an asset, for he has real ability as a festive versifier. In short, though "El tiempo vale dinero" is a truly outstanding article, Carrasquilla's limited production and his generally superficial subjects put him in the second rank of the *costumbristas*.

POMBO

Manuel Pombo (1827-1898), born in Popayán, son of a founder of the republic, was also an original member of the Mosaico group. He was graduated in law in Bogotá in 1847, lived in the Cauca for seven years, then returned to Bogotá to practice law and teach in the Universidad Nacional. Like Ricardo Silva, Pombo was apparently an amateur writer, for he himself says: "El crónico y creciente afán de mi vida, dimanante del desequilibrio entre mis presupuestos, no me dejó sosiego ni humor para permitirme esparcimientos literarios." Also according to his own testimony, he sometimes wrote in his store to escape participation in the constant, fruitless *tertulia* there. Since as a poet he was overshadowed by his brother Rafael, he is remembered primarily as a *costumbrista*, though his production is limited. The only available collection of his work is that in Volume XXVII of the Selección Samper Ortega. Most of his articles were apparently written late in life and are based on reminiscences of youth.

"La contradanza" is a romantically subjective description of a formal dance very similar to that described from a very different point of view by Caicedo Rojas in "El Duende en un baile." In the introduction Pombo represents himself as a disillusioned old man invoking memories of happier days—"Días de la juventud, ¡cómo volasteis! horas de la ilusión, ¡cuán cortas fuísteis! años del desengaño, ¡vuestra carrera es qué lenta!" Such sticky romanticism is the dominant tone of the piece. Pombo and a friend escort two sisters, whom they call Diana and Hada, to a fashionable dance, every detail of which is recorded with approving tenderness, though it could not have been greatly different from the sordid function attended by Caicedo Rojas. The author has his moment of triumph when he and his lovely Hada lead the *contradanza*, the elaborate figures of which are technically reported, and are rewarded at the end of the hour-long performance by cries of "viva el puesto." Later in the evening some of the ladies dance the *bambuco*, and there is singing to the accompaniment of guitars. The dance ends at dawn and the article concludes on the same note of nostalgic disenchantment on which it began. The value of the article is that, in spite of its preoccupation with romance and illusion, it is a complete picture of a typical dance. With the Caicedo article to counteract its sweetness, the reader can establish what is substance and what is aura.

"La guitarra," a description of a *tertulia casera* of the author's youth, is a more interesting and less cloying evocation of the "good old days." Three families, including a dozen young people, congregate in a baroque setting described in theatrical terms:

> La escena pasa en una sala con dos ventanas en el fondo hacia la calle, bastidor lateral que la comunica con la alcoba, puerta de entrada sobre el corredor. Cuatro mesas en los cuatro ángulos con sus correspondientes tocadores, perros sentados y leones dormidos de la fábrica de loza, floreros, candeleros con su vela y las despabiladoras en dos de ellas; canapés repartidos; silletas llenando los intermedios; mesa redonda en el centro con carpeta, florero y bandeja con cigarros. Láminas que representaban episodios de la Atala; retrato al óleo del dueño de la casa con casaca de gran cuello, corbatín y sellos pendientes de uno de los bolsillos del chaleco; miniatura de la señora con peinetón, bucles y mangas abombadas. Grande aseo, flores frescas, atmósfera sahumada.

The young men at first scrupulously ignore the girls and talk politely with the "personas graves," but with the arrival of the last guests the *tertulia* takes on the "fisonomía franca y festiva de las reuniones de su clase."

> ... Aquí Rosa repasaba su valse acompañada por una segunda guitarra, con intermedios de diálogos picantes; allá, en bulliciosa contienda, Dolores y dos de las Polancos, competían en chistes y agudezas con sus acompañantes. El atortolado Héctor por un lado representaba cerca de Aledaida el papel de amante corto de genio; mientras que por otro Pepita con dos adlateres aprendía pruebas en la baraja. El casero y el coronel fumaban, y leían *El Día* en el cuarto de estudio, y las mamás moralizaban a sus anchas sobre la crónica de la ciudad.

Before midnight and "aquella justamente afamada despedida de las mujeres, que es tan larga," there is dancing, and the daughters of the host entertain by singing the popular songs of the day. By way of commentary on the singing the author inserts his moral:

> Hoy su letra anticuada y su modesta música provocan el desdén de los que sólo hallan bueno lo que no pueden juzgar, la lengua extranjera y las arias y cavatinas de los encumbrados maestros, extranjeros también. Hoy todo es teatro, exhibición y fórmula, y las sabrosas cordialidades van desapareciendo.

The latter part of this article is made tedious by long and impertinent descriptions of some of the *tertulianos*, but the first part effectively conveys a warmly remembered past. It is curious that there were not more attempts by the *costumbristas* to record more or less objectively a traditional *tertulia*, and, in the absence of a better effort, Pombo's article is adequate.

Pombo's masterpiece is "La niña Agueda," in which he reconstructs from memory the home of his uncle Pepe and aunt Mariquita, where he lived as a child. Whether typical or not, this household is undeniably picturesque and amazing for its size and diversity.

> En casa de mi buena tía Mariquita había mucha gente, y por consiguiente mucho que hacer.
>
> Además de los caseros con sus seis hijos, vivían en ella: tío Bruno, dos huéspedes que se alternaban de nuestra provincia, con sus respectivos sirvientes; el maestro Guillermo y *ña* Rosa, su mujer; la niña Prima; Cecilia la expósita, siete criadas, y yo. Era un efectivo permanente de veinticuatro personas, fuera de gatos, lora, mico, mirla y completo surtido de aves de corral.

The presence of many of these persons, since she was under no obligation to them at all, testifies to the generosity of Mariquita, a handsome woman of great human sympathy, perseverance, alertness, and unusual managerial ability. In addition to her seven servants with rigidly specified duties described in detail by Pombo, Mariquita has an indispensable right arm in the management of her complicated menage in the person of *niña* Agueda, a woman of slightly more than twenty, dark, cheerful, affectionate, and pleasant looking but not pretty. Agueda, who is called *niña* because her status is too high for the *ña* and too low for *señora*, is officially the seamstress of the house, but in practice she is rather like a prime minister to Mariquita. One of the first ceremonies of every day is a conference in the sewing room during which Mariquita and Agueda "acordaban las evoluciones y maniobras que para cada caso aconsejaban la diplomacia o la estrategia, y quedaban establecidas la consigna y la orden general para el día." Pombo briefly lists some of her other endless duties and services:

> La niña Agueda repartía . . . la ropa aplanchada; escoltaba a las niñas hasta el colegio y les adornaba las muñecas; acompañaba al enfermo y lo distraía con cuentos; custodiaba en la procesión del Corpus al Sumo Sacerdote o el carro de Holofernes que se preparaba en la casa; hacía sacar las muelas a las criadas, las llevaba a confesar, fuegos y toros; . . . presidía la excursión a los cerros para traer laurel, arrayán, chite y musgo para el pesebre, de cuya construcción se encargaba; cobraba los alquileres de las tiendas; acomodaba el avío en las petacas de los huéspedes que se marchaban; era el comodín para todo lo imprevisto, y todavía en

sus momentos desocupados esta laboriosa criatura sacaba hilas para el hospital, y tenía tiempo para espulgar al mico y enseñar a hablar a la lora.

After ten years in the service of Doña Mariquita this incredibly patient and industrious woman mysteriously disappeared, to return five years later without explanation, wasted and thin. In a brief time she died, smiling, with her eyes on her crucifix.

Here again Pombo presents a valuable picture of an extinct society, a glimpse of an idyllic patriarchal order at its remembered best. Although the article is ostensibly a character sketch of Agueda, it is as much a tribute to Pombo's aunt. The portraits of these two women are excellent, and Pombo uses dialogue to good effect in sketching them, but the main interest and value of the piece are in the detailed exposition of the intricate workings of the remarkable household.

Childhood memory also provides the subject for "El maestro Custodio," a curious mixture of manners, pathos, and morality. Custodio was the tailor who made clothes for the children of Doña Mariquita's family, a tailor of "menor cuantía" whose clientele consisted exclusively of children, servants, and Indians. The tailor was a good man, but his share of life's burden was too great to bear. His alcoholic wife victimized him and their daughter mercilessly, and, ultimately, paralyzed him for life with a blow on the head and in the same drunken rage killed the daughter's mongrel dog. The daughter lost her mind from shock. Along with this pathetic narrative the article describes the tailoring of suits for the author and his brothers, their mingled joy and embarrassment when they first appear in them, and their chagrin when they are ridiculed by their friends. Though this piece does not compare with "La niña Agueda," it does successfully evoke the emotions and enthusiasm of childhood and reveals, albeit with too much pathos, that the world of Pombo's youth was not all sweetness and light.

"Los Diablitos," quite different from Pombo's reminiscent articles, is an attempt at objective description of a popular festival in Antioquia. From December 28 to 30 the city officials vacate their offices and allow their functions to be assumed by members of the lower classes. All restraint and obligation are put away for three days of revelry, and remarkably enough, says the author, this freedom from inhibition never leads to license—"la moralidad (que Dios conserve) del pueblo antioqueño, está a prueba de diversión y licor." The days of the *fiesta* are occupied with songs and dances, satirical skits, and symbolic tableaux, and the nights with dancing, singing, and drinking, and there is never a breach of order. After three days the people return with calm resignation to their normal routine. Pombo attempts here to capture the gay spirit of a picturesque festival, but the picture has no life. There are not even sufficient details for the reader to understand the physical features of the celebration. The subject seems to deserve better treatment.

Pombo's reputation as a *costumbrista* rests on the three reminiscent articles first discussed here. Though all of them have defects, "La niña Agueda" fewer than the others, they are valuable for the information they bring to an understanding of the polite manners of the 1840's. His style has at best a simple dignity and is free from mannerisms, and he has a moderate talent for description, but there is no question that his greatest gift is his power of evocation. It is perfectly obvious that, as he confesses, his principal motive in writing was "para vivir un rato más en el perdido edén de los recuerdos juveniles." The romantic disillusionment of the framework of "La contradanza" is probably feigned, but there is a gentle and sometimes too sentimental sadness in all of his articles. He offers no satire and very little overt criticism, but his implicit complaint that the simple manners of his youth no longer prevail aligns him with that school of *costumbristas* whose orientation is all toward the past. Reminiscence is his forte, and in this narrow field he is capable, but his harp has but one string. As Samper Ortega says in the introduction to his collection of Pombo's articles, he must be placed in the second rank of that "brillante pléyade" called the Mosaico.

BORDA

José Joaquín Borda (1835-1878) was born in Boyacá and educated in Bogotá. He travelled in France, Belgium, the United States, Cuba, and Perú, did diplomatic service in Venezuela, was representative to the national congress and to the provincial legislatures of Boyacá and Cundinamarca, and was a teacher and director of schools in Bogotá and in Guayaquil, Ecuador. He was one of the founders of *El Mosaico* and an editor of many other papers—*El Hogar, El Iris, La Revista de*

Bogotá, and *El Eco Literario.* He also founded *El Album* (May, 1856, to February, 1857), in which he published sketches of manners by José Manuel Groot, Ricardo Carrasquilla, and Juan Francisco Ortiz.

Laverde Amaya says there was no kind of literature at which Borda did not try his hand.[3] His poetry was romantic and he translated from Byron, Lamartine, and Ossian. In prose his models were Sainte Beuve and Larra. Aside from a collection of poetry and some unpublished dramas, his most important work is history. He edited a volume of *costumbrista* articles called *Cuadros de costumbres y descripciones locales de Colombia* (Bogotá, 1878) and, with Vergara y Vergara, *La lira granadina* (Bogotá, 1860), an anthology of Colombian poetry.

Two of Borda's few articles on manners were published in the first volume of the *Museo de cuadros de costumbres.* In one of them, a satirical piece called "Un viajero," he argues that travel, though generally an educational experience productive of understanding and tolerance, sometimes stimulates only vanity. His example is Boca-de-lobo, so called for a speech defect, a provincial youth who is a *"pobre diablo* en toda la estension de la palabra." In his journey through the taverns of England, France, and Spain he is hardly better treated than at home, although he is accorded a certain deference in France in tribute to his apparent wealth, and he feels as frustrated on his return to Colombia as he did when he left. The author finds him better dressed and cleaner—"era un completo lord"—but when he attempts to give him a welcoming embrace Boca-de-lobo exclaims, "Qué costumbres! . . . En Inglaterra eso no se hace." Borda summarizes the advantages of travel in this case:

> Nada de nuestro país le gustaba; todo lo encontraba defectuoso, malo, bárbaro i salvaje. Se habian secado en su corazón las flores del afecto i la ternura, que nacen en la infancia a los rayos del patrio sol. Un año de viaje bastó para convertirlo en el enemigo mas implacable de su patria. Si en su mano estuviera la incendiaria toda i sembraria sal en su suelo: eso es lo que se deduce de sus palabras. ¿No habria sido mejor que hubiese aprendido algo nuevo, para ponerlo al servicio de su patria? Las maldiciones qué dejan?

This article is rather like Juan Francisco Ortiz' "El viaje de don Pascualito" and may owe something to Larra's "En este

---

[3] *Bibliografía colombiana* (Bogotá: Imprenta y Librería de Medardo Rivas, 1895), p. 76.

país," in which an eminently unqualified critic is violently critical of his country. Borda's thesis is weakened by emphasizing the physical defect of his Boca-de-lobo, who, in fact, was already worthless before his exposure to travel. He apparently tries to give the boy some positive qualities but they fail to come out clearly. The article is capably written, but as satire it is not very effective.

"Seis horas en un champan" is a descriptive account of a trip on the Magdalena River. The *champan* is a thirty- or forty-foot boat, manned by a dozen or more half-savage oarsmen of mixed blood, which was Bogotá's only access to the Atlantic until the arrival of the steamboat in 1845. Borda, during his short trip to the southernmost port accessible to the steamboat, devotes much attention to the savage and imposing aspects of the landscape and the nature and habits of the oarsmen, and he successfully avoids romantic idealization in both cases. His picture seems realistic and authentic in both detail and atmosphere.

Borda published over the pseudonym *Mudarra,* in a number of *El Mosaico* (December 8, 1860) given exclusively to prose and verse tributes to the Virgin, an article called "Fiestas de la Virgen de Chiquinquirá." He opens with the declaration that it is next to impossible to describe the *fiesta* in all the color and exactness it demands, and his effort does not disprove the assertion. He includes a long and laborious description of the miraculous image of the Virgin from an unidentified document of 1735, dismisses very briefly the celebrations called *Rosarios* of the week preceding the Virgin's day, and describes even more summarily the climactic rites on December 17. The last part of the article consists of pious commonplaces on the healthfulness of this cult of the Virgin. The reader does glean the interesting data that as many as fifty thousand people attended the *fiesta* and that the image was twice carried as far as Bogotá, once in 1633 and again in 1840, the year of a devastating smallpox epidemic. The article, which must have been written hastily to order, has little color or distinction and a great deal of confusion and digression.

Borda does better in "El último Corpus en Bogotá" (*El Mosaico,* June 13, 1860). He opens with a lament that each year the celebration seems a little less brilliant than the year before.

Dónde están ya las ricas colgaduras de damasco i cachemira que en otro tiempo ornaban puertas, balcones i ventanas? dónde la pintada lluvia de flores que de estas i de aquellos volaban entapizando el suelo i aromatizando el ambiente? dónde los antiguos carros de *ninfas* con sus Salomones i sus Judides i sus Holoférnes de siete años? Dónde los colorines de los dandys, la seda de las hermosas i las anchas frisas bayeta-Edwars de las rollizas criadas? dónde los ricos arcos (¡formados de ángulos rectos!) en los cuales brillaban en amistosa comparsa los espejos i los retratos de Napoleon i Bolívar, con las viñetas de santos i de lindas bailarinas? dónde las revendedoras sentadas, con mas orgullo que un rei sobre su trono, entre inmensos cestos de frutas? dónde los entorchados i las franjas coloradas de los fieles servidores de la patria, de los hijos de Belona? dónde en fin, ese ruido, ese entusiasmo, esa vida incógnita i nueva que ántes circulaba, sin poder ser cojida, sin saberse en dónde estaba, pero sentida de todos, como el color i la luz?

The procession this year, says Borda, passed through streets almost empty of spectators, although the hour was not unduly early. But, in spite of the absence of the color and spirit of other days, the occasion did have attractions, for present on the balconies were those mysterious beauties who allow themselves to be seen in public only two or three times a year, and the young men in the streets and cafés were no less boisterous than those of earlier generations. So the great festival of Corpus Christi, though languishing, was hardly dead. Here, as in the preceding article, distinguishing details in description are not numerous, but Borda does add to the portrayals of the Corpus by other authors and even captures something of the holiday spirit.

Borda's scanty work as a *costumbrista* does not rank with the best in Colombia. "Un viajero" is probably the best of his articles, but, although it treats a likely subject for satire, the effect is disappointing. He shows some descriptive gift in "Seis horas en un champan," which from the point of view of information is his greatest contribution to the archive of Colombian manners, but he does not follow through in the two articles on popular *fiestas*. All of his work seems to have been done in haste and with little care.

SAMPER

José María Samper (1828-1888) was a man of tremendous energy who, according to Otero Muñoz, left an indelible mark on the thought and literature of his day.

Las doctrinas políticas y literarias se renovaron al influjo de su obra. Se rebeló contra los resabios coloniales que aun predominaban a mediados del siglo último en nuestra sociedad, pero fecundando el ideal revolucionario de justicia y progreso con un nuevo sentimiento de la libertad, propicio al arte y a la democracia americanos.[4]

Samper was alleged to be a free-thinker and a Benthamist utilitarian until a series of political disappointments and the shock of his mother's death led him in 1865 to a reconversion to orthodox Catholicism, after which his liberalism was somewhat dampened although he continued to campaign for common sense in politics and real constitutional government.

He was born in Honda and educated in Bogotá, where he took a degree in law at the age of eighteen. He entered politics at twenty, served in the congress several times, held diplomatic posts in Chile and Argentina, and in his late years had judicial office. In 1858 he went to Europe, where he stayed five years, wrote for Bogotá, Lima, and Madrid newspapers, and published five books.

Samper's journalistic career began with the publication of an article in *El Día* when he was fifteen. During his lifetime he edited or helped to edit a dozen newspapers, including *El Arbor Literario* (1845), the first exclusively literary paper in Colombia, and two papers in Lima. He was an important member of the Mosaico group in spite of frequent and long absences from Bogotá and meetings were often held at his home. As an author he was both versatile and prolific. His works include novels (Otero Muñoz lists nine), plays, several volumes of verse and essays, and treatises on history, government, sociology, travel, and biography. Unhappily, very little of his work fits the *costumbrista* classification.

In "Literatura fósil," which appeared in 1864 in *El Mosaico*, Samper puts his finger satirically on a real evil in Spanish American writing, the over-worked cliché. He examines the character and writing of a journalist named Modesto Pichón, a man of influence in literature and politics, determined to find the secret of his success. Samper finds his political articles saturated with stereotyped phrases and tired metaphors:

> Una *nueva aurora alumbra nuestro horizonte político;* una *nueva era comienza* en los fastos de nuestra historia. *De hoy más, la hidra de la discordia no levantará su cabeza.* El *timón del Estado*

---

[4] José María Samper, *Un alcalde a la antigua* (Selección Samper Ortega de Literatura Colombiana, Vol. XCIV), p. 5.

estará en manos de *un hábil piloto*, que no dejará *zozobrar la nave de la República, azotada por contrarios vientos.* . . .

Having studied Pichón's work, Samper comes to this conclusion about him:

> Profundamente ignorante del fondo de las cosas, por falta de verdadero talento, estudio y método, sin embargo, algunas lecturas superficiales, el trato con el mundo, la memoria de las palabras, y sobre todo su admirable desparpajo, le habían hecho adquirir cierto caudal de sofismas, frases tradicionales, citas y lugares comunes; variedades de algas parásitas que viven en las aguas de la literatura sin razón de ser, porque sobrenadan en esa espuma inestinguible que se llama el *hábito*. A fuerza de remendar frases, cebándose como un cuervo en los despojos de la literatura *fósil*, que los cataclismos del tiempo han dejado a flor de tierra, Modesto había pelechado, ganado fama y subido a la categoría de personaje.

Then, speaking in general terms, Samper remarks the inconsistency that, in a Spanish America which has been able to liberate itself politically and to some degree socially, literature, still languishing at the crossroads of plagiarism and bad taste, has been unable to free itself from commonness. A long list of clichés indispensable to the work-kit of the journalist follows. By way of conclusion, Samper makes two proposals to correct the evil personified by Pichón.

> O hagamos una inmensa pira con todos esos mamotretos, esa leña podrida que nos viene por herencia de los siglos, y metámosle fuego con cartuchos de necrologías, felicitaciones, proclamas militares, programas gubernamentales y otras variedades mentirosas;
>
> O fundemos un gran museo de paleontología literaria; releguemos a sus armarios todas las ruinas del ingenio, entre las cuales vivirá el mal gusto como un viejo lagarto, y escribamos en el frontispicio: "Depósito de literatura fósil: se admite gratis toda la que se traiga."

This article, perceptive and penetrating in its criticism and forceful and imaginative in its style, effectively supports Otero Muñoz' notion of Samper as a revivifying force in Colombian letters.

In "El triunvirato parroquial" Samper turns his analytic eye to rural politics and government, which he sees as a great cancer at the heart of the "democratic" system in an "época que por hábito o buena crianza llamamos republicana." The introduction is interesting for its expression of Samper's idea of the *costumbrista's* calling. While José David Guarín, in his "San Isidro Labrador," sets forth the mission of the *costumbrista* as a recorder of contemporary history, Samper sees him as a critic who must expect and accept with resignation public wrath and denunciation. Many *costumbristas* complain petulantly of abuse by those they criticize, but Samper holds that the critic of manners is a purposeful reformer for whom censure is inevitable.

> Escribir para el público es una locura como cualquiera otra, cuyos percances es preciso aceptar con tranquila conformidad. Un escritor sincero y desinteresado es un camorrista sublime. No es posible hacer tortillas sin quebrar los huevos, dice un adagio francés; y puesto que el diablo nos tienta y su compañía nos agrada, fuerza es que llevemos en el pellejo las señales de sus uñas. . . . Si logramos nuestro fin, que es bosquejar corrigiendo, sin fastidiar al que nos lea, tanto mejor; si encallamos, lluevan sobre nosotros bofetones y palos, que en esta materia el más dichoso es aquel que posee gordas mejillas y sólidas espaldas.

If more Colombian *costumbristas* had had Samper's "strong back," plus his critical perception, the genre would have been enriched.

The *triunvirato parroquial* which is the subject of the article is composed of the *gamonal*, the *tinterillo*, and the *párroco*, who are the executive, judicial, and legislative powers of the rural community.

> . . . Se llama "gamonal," (por no decir capataz o cacique) al hombre rico de un lugar pequeño, dueño o poseedor de las tierras más valiosas, especie de señor feudal de la parroquia republicana, que influye y domina soberanamente en el distrito, maneja a sus arrendatarios como a borregos, ata y desata los negocios del terruño como un San Pedro en caricatura, y dragonea sin rival entre sus coparroquianos como un gallo entre sus gallinas. El gamonal es, pues, el sátrapa de la parroquia, *el gallo del pueblo* con todas sus consecuencias.
>
> El *tinterillo* . . . es el rábula o leguleyo de parroquia, abogado de contrabando y de asuntos de menor cuantía, como quien dice, una peseta de *esterilla* en el foro. El hábito que tiene de andar de arriba a abajo con su pluma de ganso detrás de la oreja, un rollo de papel sellado sobre el ala del sombrero, y su terrible cuanto inescrutable tinterito en la faltriquera, ha inducido también a nuestros pueblos a bautizar al personaje con el nombre genérico de "tinterillo." Para poner un nombre, con gráfica y socarrona habilidad, no hay quien lo valga como un pueblo escaldado que sabe dónde le aprieta la clavija.

The priest, according to Samper, is the key figure of the trio, for a good priest may, to a degree and for a limited time, lessen or assuage the injustices of the other two. Ultimately, however, the latter are certain to prevail. Though one must not take literally, Samper warns, the poetic language of American constitutions about the sovereignty of the people and the separation of powers, he acknowledges that these principles occasionally are respected for short periods on a national level. However,

> ... en la humilde esfera de la parroquia la constitución es casi un mito, una triste superfetación. Allí, por lo común, las "garantías" son un mero *lapsus calami* escapado del pupitre de los redactores del "Cuadernito," y los poderes residen, en puridad de verdad, en el consabido triunvirato.

The article describes the injustices and indignities to which the people are subjected and explains the means by which the unholy triumvirate perpetuates its reign and avoids discovery by higher authority. The remedy for this dark state of affairs, says Samper, is "Luz! luz! muchísima luz! una inundación de luz! Y movimiento, interminable y poderoso movimiento!" Schools, highways, and conscientious and educated priests will eliminate the ignorance that allows the growth and prosperity of the *triunvirato parroquial*.

In both of these articles Samper shows the true reformer's zeal, and it is significant of his vision, though it makes him less *costumbrista*, that he means his criticism not for Colombia alone but for Spanish America in general. He writes vigorously and intensely, calling "pan pan y vino vino," and shows a true sense of democratic values. He also demonstrates real ability as a satirist by making excellent use of invective, epithet, and vivid satirical metaphors. His orientation toward the future is particularly refreshing. While he condemns an imperfect present, he feels no nostalgia for a less confused but no less imperfect past, and he implies confidence in progress and the perfectability of human institutions. Samper is a minor *costumbrista* only for his limited production. His greater participation in the genre would surely have enriched it.

THE MOSAICOS

Acknowledging again the arbitrary nature of the division of the mid-century *costumbristas* into pre-Mosaicos and Mosaicos, and even some overlapping in chronology, a few comparative observations may yet be valid.

The latter period boasts a greater number of competent authors in the big four of Vergara, Marroquín, Guarín, and Silva. There seems to be some indication that they wrote with a greater respect for the genre and hence with more care, especially in plan and organization; but they are still prone to hasty improvisation. Another difference is more apparent—under the Mosaicos the satirical-critical *artículo* lost ground to the descriptive *cuadro* and the purely humorous personal essay. Hardly more than a third of the articles by the Mosaico writers are predominantly satirical, and the satirical character sketch used so effectively by the pre-Mosaico Rivas is largely neglected; Guarín's "Un sabio parroquial" is the only first-rate specimen. The best satirist of the group is Marroquín, especially in his later articles.

Though a lessening interest in satire is in one sense an indication of declining vigor, the number of articles published and the apparent interest in them do not imply a general diminution of vitality. To compensate for their neglect of satire the most able and prolific writers developed the descriptive article to a level of quality only suggested by the earlier writers. Among the pre-Mosaico *cuadros* only Restrepo's "Mi compadre Facundo" can compare with Marroquín's "Vamos a misa al pueblo," Vergara's "Las tres tazas," "El lenguaje de las casas," and "El correísta," Silva's "El niño Agapito," and Guarín's "La camisa calentana," to cite only a few titles.

There is a symptom of effeteness in the movement more damaging than its declining interest in satire. It is the spread of the nostalgic fixation on reminiscence particularly noted in the works of Santander and Groot among the pre-Mosaicos. Pombo is most typical of the nostalgic attitude in the Mosaicos, but even the best writers are too often subject to it, and only Samper, a part-time *costumbrista*, is wholly free from it. This nostalgia, combined with a sometimes petulant intolerance of all contemporary deviation from tradition, implies a denial of milieu unhealthful for the *costumbrista* movement.

V
REVIEW AND APPRAISAL

The first *costumbrista* sketch in Colombia, a satirical-humorous essay called "Fiestas," appeared in *El Argos* as a letter to the editor in 1838. Early in 1839 Rufino Cuervo contributed to the same paper "Un representante al congreso de 1837," which some have considered the earliest Colombian specimen of *costumbrismo*. More important to the development of the genre than either of these early sketches was a series of articles written by Ignacio Gutiérrez Vergara for *El Observador* in 1839 and 1840 which established the *costumbrista* sketch as a standard journalistic feature.

In the next two decades literary magazines such as *El Duende*, *El Album*, and *El Neogranadino* flourished and the number of writers on manners increased. Santander's contribution was slight. Caicedo Rojas, Groot, and Ortiz were predominantly writers of descriptive *cuadros,* and Restrepo and Rivas, who dominate the period in vigor and quantity of production, were primarily satirists. The following twenty years were the era of the Mosaicos, who edited the curious and remarkable magazine called *El Mosaico*. In this period, in which emphasis shifted somewhat from satire to description, a number of capable writers brought the sketch of manners to its greatest popularity. By 1880 most of the Mosaicos were inactive, and from then until the end of the century the *costumbrista* genre declined, only two or three writers achieving prominence during that time.

It seems clear that Colombian *costumbrismo* originated under the influence of the Spanish movement, represented primarily by Larra and Mesonero Romanos. Announcements in newspapers and the testimony of writers and critics show that the works of Larra and Mesonero were available and popular in Colombia by 1840. Colombian articles from the early "Fiestas" show the influence of Spain, and many Colombian pieces can be associated with specific articles by Larra or Mesonero, but it is not necessary to seek evidence of close imitation to establish the Colombians' debt to Spain. Several writers acknowledge their obligation and no author claims independence from Spanish influence. Even the names of some papers—*El Observador, El Duende*—indicate the close relationship. In both Spain and

Colombia the *costumbrista* movement was born with strong satirical and critical characteristics, but as it grew and spread it became less corrective and more descriptive, emphasizing the preservation for posterity of unusual or picturesque scenes, institutions, or individuals associated with the national character. This change of emphasis came in Spain about 1845, and in Colombia ten to fifteen years later.

The favorite form of the Colombian *costumbrista* was the personal essay, nearly always humorous, sometimes farcical, in which the writer is the protagonist whose experiences or misadventures reflect or comment on society, manners, or individuals. This form, an easy and logical means of achieving the informality demanded by the genre, was used in Colombia as a vehicle for satire, description, or mere humorous exposition and narrative. A personal element is often present even in the more objective character sketch or satirical type sketch, and the purely objective, third-person narrative or descriptive article is rare. The least personal of the important sketch writers was Juan de Dios Restrepo (Emiro Kastos), and he is also the least *costumbrista*.

The personal element natural to the manners genre frequently took the character of romantic subjectivity, particularly in the articles of the Mosaico period which nostalgically indulge in reminiscence, idealizing a fading patriarchal and quasi-feudalistic past. Vergara succinctly spoke for most of his colleagues when he wrote, "Qué triste es quedarse uno poco a poco atrás!" The appraisal of Germán Arciniegas, one of Colombia's most brilliant contemporary writers and critics, is less wistful:

> ... Espíritus enfermos de una futura nostalgia, añorando costumbres que todavía estaban frescas y lozanas, y que no desaparecerían en años, enamorados de una tradición de nada, eran como la sombra del conquistador que vagaba y divagaba por sus campos sin querer abandonarlos ni traspasados ya los términos de la vida.[1]

Of all the Colombian *costumbristas* perhaps only Rivas, Restrepo, and Samper were wholly untouched by this latter-day *mal du siècle*. Whether their malady was real or imagined, the general backward orientation of the *costumbrista* writers, and the accompanying contempt for the ungraceful efforts of their contemporaries to keep pace with the world, is monotonous.

In spite of the fact that the second era of its development is

---

[1] *El libro de Santa Fe* (Bogotá: Librería Colombiana, 1929), pp. xiii-xiv.

dominated by the reminiscent and descriptive *cuadro*, Colombian *costumbrismo* has a strong satiric tradition. Most of the earliest examples of the genre were satirical, and in the pre-Mosaico period Restrepo and Rivas, and sometimes Caicedo Rojas and Juan Francisco Ortiz, continued the critical sketch with distinction. Restrepo, one of the most perceptive and capable writers of the movement, was probably the best satirist of all, but his techniques did not always conform to the demands of *costumbrismo*. Rivas was unquestionably the master of the satirical type sketch, and his series of articles is one of the high spots of the Colombian genre. In the Mosaico period Marroquín, in his articles on ostentation, continued the general satirical tradition most successfully, and two or three of Ricardo Silva's later articles show satiric vigor and talent, whereas the satire of Guarín and Carrasquilla is superficial. As an indication of the attitude of the *costumbristas* themselves and later critics toward satire as a *costumbrista* function, it may be observed that the articles most often reprinted, those considered the classics of the genre, are predominantly non-satirical. This, combined with the neglect of the very capable work of Medardo Rivas, leads to the conclusion that Colombians, critics and writers alike, have considered *costumbrismo* a primarily descriptive and humorous genre.

In style the Colombian *costumbristas* are generally undistinguished. Most of them, at least part of the time, wrote carelessly and hastily. Marroquín, who was not guilty of heedless composition, recognized this shortcoming:

> Los que han compuesto piezas de aquel género sólo por el prurito de escribir y de aumentar de cualquier modo el número de sus producciones, o apremiados por el impresor, que les exige para mañana, o para el lunes, o para el miércoles, materiales bastantes para llenar cinco columnas y media del número tal del periódico en que so han comprometido a colaborar, no han podido, por más talento y fecundidad que tengan, pintar cuadros que parezcan verdadera copia de escenas y costumbres reales.[2]

But, although many writers took advantage of the levity and informality of the genre, some authors and some articles have spots of good writing. Marroquín is conspicuous for a leisurely, rich, *castizo* style which may have been inspired in Cervantes; Restrepo at his best approaches the incisiveness of Larra; Silva is precise and correct, though not highly imaginative;

---

[2] "Prólogo" of Ricardo Silva's *Artículos de costumbres*, p. x.

and Vergara often achieves a suggestive compactness. Even Guarín, who was by no means correct or careful, has an effervescence of great charm. On the whole, however, the level of artistry is hardly better than ordinary.

The informality of the *costumbrista* sketch led to other defects than those of style. In some cases, fascinated by the opportunity to write casually and publish quickly, the *costumbristas* seemed to consider mere writing an end in itself. This led to the overuse of insipid formulae—flippant asides to the reader and cute apologies for subject and treatment, for example. Poor organization, indiscriminate digression, treatment of two or more heterogeneous subjects in one article, and undue reliance on pathos and sentimentality were other common abuses. All of these defects reflect a naiveté in literary criteria to be expected in an isolated society of little sophistication, but, although they are characteristic, it must be emphasized that they are not typical of all the Colombian writers.

Humor is an important feature of Colombian *costumbrismo*; in fact, the Colombians seem to insist more on it than did their Spanish predecessors. However, Javier Arango Ferrer, a capable and realistic critic, questions the success of their efforts to be funny:

> El género costumbrista . . . está en la escuela santafereña ocupado por la infantería ligera del buen humor; pero el humorismo, que nada tiene de común con el epigrama, es menos frecuente. Chispazos acumulados no dan humorismo.[3]

His charge is largely true. There is no question that for many *costumbristas* humor meant stringing jokes together without regard for their pertinence and much of what was intended primarily as humor does not amuse today. Juan Francisco Ortiz' "Motivo por el cual," to cite one example, is a *tour de force* of grotesque situations and interpolated jokes which belie its reputation as a funny piece. But, in spite of the general truth of Arango Ferrer's assertion, truly humorous and witty articles can be found. Carrasquilla's "El tiempo vale dinero" is an excellent example of whimsy; real wit is present in Marroquín's "Los diminutivos" and "Vamos a misa al pueblo," Rivas' "Contrariedades de un redactor" and "El comerciante," and Vergara's "Esquina de avisos"; there is effective humor of situation in Silva's "Ponga usted tienda" and "El remiendito," as well

---

[3] *La literatura de Colombia* (Las Literaturas Americanas, Vol. III; Buenos Aires: Imprenta y Casa Editora "Coni," 1940), p. 70.

as in Marroquín's "Penitencia"; and humor of character is plentiful in Silva's "El niño Agapito" and Guarín's "La camisa calentana." All the *costumbristas*, even the atrabilious Restrepo, tried to be festive on occasion, and many of them were often thwarted by the very effort. The most consistently humorous of them all was probably Guarín, whose greatest virtue is his irrepressible insouciance.

Although the Colombian *costumbrista* movement was not an unqualified success in satire, style, general artistry, or humor, it leaves little to be desired in the scope of its subject matter. No single author systematically chronicles an entire society, as did Mesonero in Madrid, but the sum of the efforts of the many Colombian writers is a complete panorama of their environment. Even a partial list of their subjects is imposing: manners of fashionable society, folk customs and festivals, political practices, economic conditions and business practices, legal and governmental procedures, national psychology, country life and farm methods, religious customs, servant types and problems, burial and mourning practices, marriage, education, domestic life, vacations and diversions, travel, foreign influence on manners, social functions, sartorial fashions, public morality, houses and lodging, speech habits, problems of earning a living, doctors and medicines, journalism, literary tastes, and people of all classes and types. This mass of material is especially eloquent in revealing the hardship and anguish of life in an atmosphere of almost constant political unrest and revolution, although these subjects are seldom dealt with directly. Whatever other criticism may be appropriate, it is undeniable that the Colombian *costumbristas* expose the countenance and soul of their society, and in so doing they accomplish one of the major purposes of the genre of manners.

In final appraisal of the Colombian *costumbrista* movement it is interesting and useful to consider the opinions of two Colombian critics, both scholarly and capable. Gustavo Otero Muñoz is enthusiastic:

> Por entonces [1859] se hallaba el costumbrismo colombiano en pleno apogeo, y desde las columnas de la *Biblioteca de Señoritas* y *El Mosaico*, irradiaban las plumas de Vergara y Vergara, Carrasquilla, Borda, Marroquín, Caicedo Rojas, Eugenio Díaz y David Guarín, con resplandores que marcarían la época más sólida de nuestra literatura.[4]

---

[4] *Resumen de historia de literatura colombiana*, p. 139.

Javier Arango Ferrer is sardonically skeptical:
> Es posible que *El Mosaico* haya sido el movimiento más interesante del realismo en América, como afirman algunos críticos: esto quiere decir que en los demás países, el género fué todavía más intrascendente.[5]

As might be expected in a world of compromise, a truly reasonable evaluation lies between these two extremes. Although the movement offers no transcendental contribution to world literature or thought, it accomplished in large measure the purpose of this minor genre. Perhaps no greater tribute can be paid the *costumbrista* writers of mid-century Colombia than to testify that there is very little of their work which cannot be read with interest a hundred years after it was written.

---

[5] *La literatura de Colombia*, pp. 71-72.

Bibliography

Works of Reference

Arango Ferrer, Javier. *La literatura de Colombia*. Las Literaturas Americanas, Vol. III. Buenos Aires: Imprenta y Casa Editora "Coni," 1940.

Archbold, Juliana E. "The *Costumbrista* Sketch in Colombia, 1858-1872." Unpublished Master's Thesis, Duke University, 1947.

Carrasquilla, Ricardo. "Apuntes para mi biografía," *Santafé y Bogotá*, IV (1924), 168-169.

Gómez Restrepo, Antonio. *Bogotá. La literatura colombiana a mediados del siglo XIX. Dos ensayos*. [Ediciones Colombia, Vol. XX] Bogotá: [Talleres de Ediciones Colombia], 1926.

———. "La literatura colombiana," *Revue Hispanique*, XLIII (1918), 79-204.

Henao, Jesús María, and Gerardo Arrubla. *History of Colombia*. Translated and edited by J. Fred Rippy. Chapel Hill: University of North Carolina Press, 1938.

Larra, Mariano José de. *Obras completas de Fígaro*. Vols. I and III. Paris: Garnier Hermanos, n.d.

Laverde Amaya, Isidoro. *Bibliografía colombiana*. Vol. I. Bogotá: Imprenta y Librería de Medardo Rivas, 1895. Only one volume published, A-O.

———. *Fisonomías literarias de Colombia*. Curaçao: Bethencourt e Hijos, 1890.

Leavitt, Sturgis E., and Carlos García-Prada. *A Tentative Bibliography of Colombian Literature*. Harvard Council. Cambridge: Harvard University Press, 1934.

Marroquín, José Manuel. "De la neografía en América y particularmente en Colombia," *Repertorio Colombiano*, II (1879), 403-425.

———. *Retórica y poética*. Selección Samper Ortega de Literatura Colombiana, Vol. IV. 3d ed. Bogotá: Editorial Minerva, 1935.

Marroquín, José Manuel, Presbítero. *Don José Manuel Marroquín íntimo*. Bogotá: Arboleda y Valencia, 1915.

———. "Revolviendo papeles," *Santafé y Bogotá*, VIII (1926), 180-183, 200-203, 269-271.

[Mesonero Romanos, Ramón de]. *Panorama matritense*. Primera serie de las escenas, 1832 a 1835, por el Curioso Parlante. [Madrid]: Oficinas de la Ilustración Española y Americana, 1881.

Montgomery, Clifford Marvin. *Early Costumbrista Writers in Spain, 1750-1830*. Philadelphia: [University of Pennsylvania], 1931.

Otero Muñoz, Gustavo. "El costumbrismo en Colombia," *Santafé y Bogotá*, XIII (1930), 355-358, 401-403.

———. *Historia del periodismo en Colombia*. Selección Samper Ortega de Literatura Colombiana, Vol. LXI. Bogotá: Editorial Minerva, n.d.

———. *Resumen de historia de la literatura colombiana*. 4th ed. Bogotá: Librería Voluntad, 1943.

Samper, José María. "Discurso de recepción en la Academia Colombiana," *Repertorio Colombiano*, XII (1886), 52-81.

Tarr, F. Courtney. "Romanticism in Spain and Spanish Romanticism," *Bulletin of Spanish Studies*, XVI (1939), 3-37.
Vergara y Vergara, José María. *Historia de la literatura en Nueva Granada desde la conquista hasta la independencia (1538-1820). Obras escogidas*, IV and V. Bogotá: Editorial Minerva, 1931.

COLLECTIONS

[Arciniegas, Germán (ed.)]. *El libro de Santa Fe. Los cuadros de costumbres, las crónicas, las leyendas bogotanas de hace un siglo.* Ediciones Colombia. [Bogotá]: Librería Colombiana, 1929.
Borda, José Joaquín (ed.). *Cuadros de costumbres y descripciones locales de Colombia.* Bogotá: Librería y Papelería de F. García Rico, 1878.
Caicedo Rojas, José. *Apuntes de ranchería, noticias biográficas y artículos varios. Escritos escogidos.* I. Bogotá: Zalamea Hermanos, 1885.
――――, Rafael Eliseo Santander, and Juan Francisco Ortiz. *Cuadros de costumbres.* Selección Samper Ortega de Literatura Colombiana, Vol. XXII. 3d ed. Bogotá: Editorial Minerva, n.d.
Carrasquilla, Ricardo. *Obras.* Bogotá: Imprenta de "La Luz," 1927.
Díaz, Eugenio. *Una ronda de Don Ventura Ahumada, y otros cuadros.* Selección Samper Ortega de Literatura Colombiana, Vol. XXIII. 3d ed. Bogotá: Editorial Minerva, n.d.
Groot, José Manuel. *Cuadros de costumbres.* Selección Samper Ortega de Literatura Colombiana, Vol. XXI. 3d ed. Bogotá: Editorial Minerva, n.d.
――――. *Dios y patria. Artículos escogidos.* Bogotá: Casa Editorial de Medardo Rivas, 1894.
Guarín, José David. *Artículos y novelas.* Socorro: Imprenta del Estado, 1872.
――――. *Obras.* Bogotá: Imprenta de Zalamea Hermanos, 1880.
――――. *Una docena de pañuelos, y otros* [sic]. Selección Samper Ortega de Literatura Colombiana, Vol. XXVI, 3d ed. Bogotá: Editorial Minerva, n.d.
Kastos, Emiro. *See* Restrepo.
Marroquín, José Manuel. *Artículos literarios.* Literatura Colombiana, Vol. I. Bogotá: Librería Santa Fe, 1920.
――――. *Nada nuevo. Historias, cuentos y otros escritos viejos.* Bogotá: Librería Americana, 1908.
[Navarro, Nepomuceno J., and José David Guarín (eds.)]. *Lirios y azucenas. Colección de producciones literarias de los más distinguidos literatos de Colombia.* Socorro: Imprenta del Estado, 1871.
Ortiz, Juan Francisco. *See* Caicedo Rojas.
Pombo, Manuel. *La niña Agueda y otros cuadros.* Selección Samper Ortega de Literatura Colombiana, Vol. XXVII. 3d ed. Bogotá: Editorial Minerva, n.d.
――――. *Obras inéditas.* Bogotá: Imprenta de "La Tribuna," 1914.
Restrepo, Juan de Dios (Emiro Kastos). *Colección de artículos escogidos.* Bogotá: Imprenta de Pizano y Pérez, 1859.
――――. *Mi compadre Facundo y otros cuadros.* Selección Samper Ortega de

Literatura Colombiana, Vol. XXIX. 3d ed. Bogotá: Editorial Minerva, n.d.

Rivas, Medardo. *Obras. Parte primera, novelas, artículos de costumbres, variedades, poesías.* Bogotá: Fernando Pontón, 1883.

Santander, Rafael Eliseo. See Caicedo Rojas.

Silva, Ricardo. *Artículos de costumbres.* Bogotá: Imprenta de Silvestre, 1883.

———. *Un domingo en casa y otros cuadros.* Selección Samper Ortega de Literatura Colombiana, Vol. XXV. 3d ed. Bogotá: Editorial Minerva, n.d.

Vergara y Vergara, José María. *Obras escogidas.* Vol. I, *Cuadros de costumbres.* Vol. II, *Artículos literarios.* Bogotá: Editorial Minerva, 1931.

———. *Las tres tazas y otros cuadros.* Selección Samper Ortega de Literatura Colombiana, Vol. XXIV. 3d ed. Bogotá: Editorial Minerva, n.d.

[——— (ed.)] *Museo de cuadros. de costumbres.* Biblioteca de "El Mosaico." 2 vols. Bogotá: Foción Mantilla, 1866. (Title of second volume reads: *Museo de cuadros de costumbres i variedades.*)

PERIODICALS

El Album. Bogotá, 1856-1857.
El Argos. Bogotá, 1837-1839.
La Biblioteca de Señoritas. Bogotá, 1858-1859.
El Cachaco de Bogotá. Bogotá, 1833-1834.
El Correo. Bogotá, 1839-1840.
El Día. Bogotá, 1840-1851.
El Duende. Bogotá, 1846-1847.
El Hogar. Bogotá, 1868-1870.
El Mosaico. Bogotá, 1858-1865.
El Neogranadino. Bogotá, 1848-1857.
El Observador. Bogotá, 1839-1840.
Papel Periódico Ilustrado. Bogotá, 1881-1888.
El Pasatiempo. Bogotá, 1851-1854.
El Pueblo. Medellín, 1855-1857.
El Repertorio Colombiano. Bogotá, 1878-1899.
El Tiempo. Bogotá, 1855-1872.
El Trovador. Bogotá, 1850.

www.ingramcontent.com/pod-product-compliance
Lightning Source LLC
Chambersburg PA
CBHW030237240426
43663CB00037B/1240